Panzerjäger: Tank Hunter

Panzerjäger: Tank Hunter

William B. Folkestad

Burd Street Press

All illustrations are from the collection of Bernhard Averbeck.

This Burd Street Press publication
was printed by
Beidel Printing House, Inc.
63 West Burd Street
Shippensburg, PA 17257-0152 USA

In respect for the scholarship contained herein, the acid-free paper used in this book meets the guidelines for permanence and durability of the Committee on Production Guidelines for Book Longevity of the Council on Library Resources.

For a complete list of available publications
please write
Burd Street Press
Division of White Mane Publishing Company, Inc.
P.O. Box 152
Shippensburg, PA 17257-0152 USA

Library of Congress Cataloging-in-Publication Data

Averbeck, Bernhard, 1924–
Panzerjäger : tank hunter / [as told to] William B. Folkestad.
p. cm.
ISBN 1-57249-074-8 (alk. paper)
1. Averbeck, Bernhard, 1924– 2. World War, 1939–1945--Personal narratives, German. 3. Germany. Heer. Panzerjäger Abteilung, 195- -History. 4. Soldiers--Germany--Biography. 5. Germany. Heer- -Biography. I. Folkestad, William B., 1955– . II. Title.
D811.A777 1997
940.54'21'092--dc21
[B] 97-27305
CIP

PRINTED IN THE UNITED STATES OF AMERICA

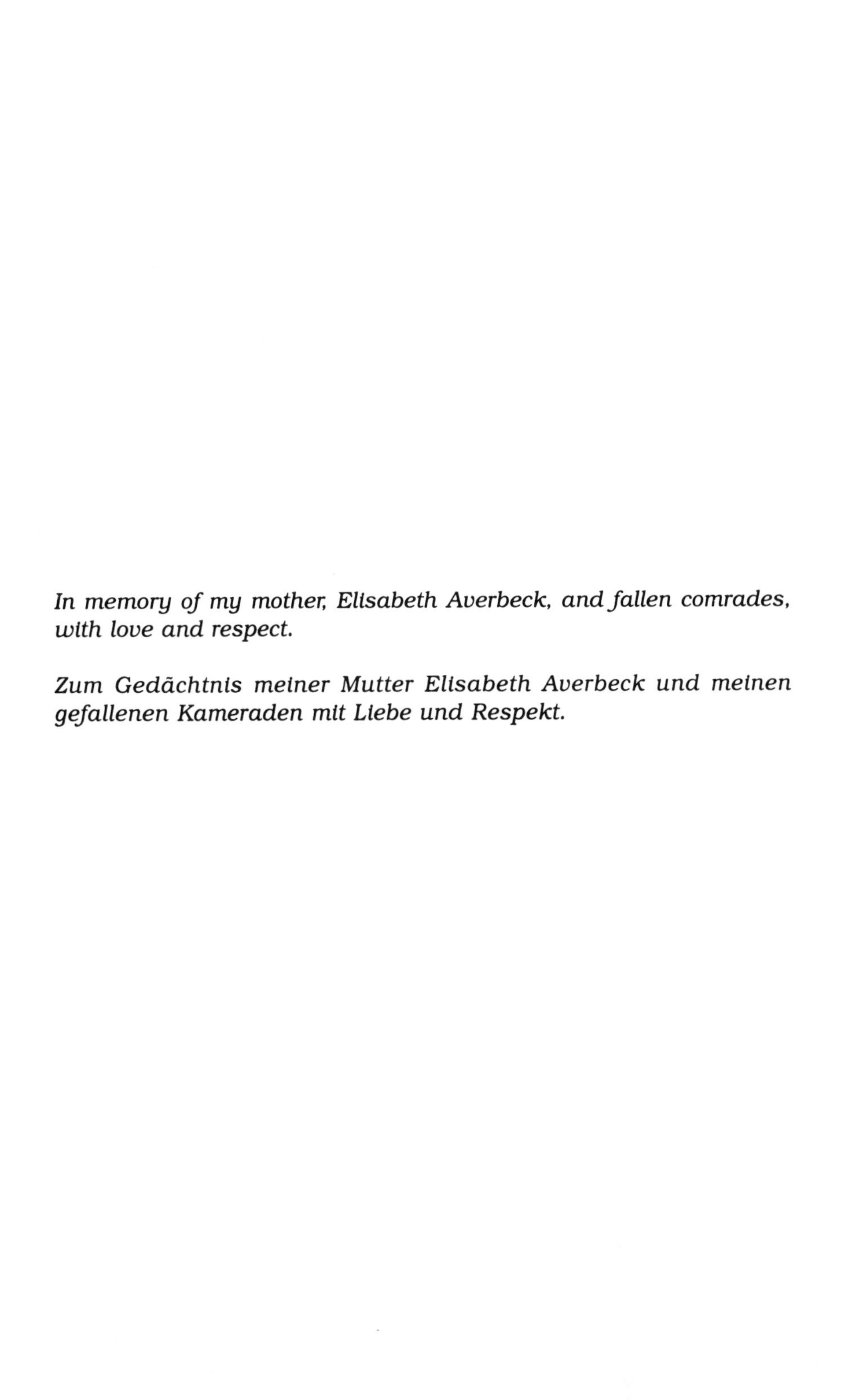

In memory of my mother, Elisabeth Averbeck, and fallen comrades, with love and respect.

Zum Gedächtnis meiner Mutter Elisabeth Averbeck und meinen gefallenen Kameraden mit Liebe und Respekt.

Table of Contents

Illustrations

Preface

Panzerjäger: Tank Hunter is Bernhard Averbeck's true account of his experiences fighting with various *Panzerjäger* units between 1942 and 1944 on the Eastern Front and from 1944 to 1945 on the Western Front. This is the first book in English personalizing German antitank warfare.

Men like Averbeck represented the largest group of combatants to serve in any of the German theaters of World War II: the soldier without military, political or family motives. His views are those of any eighteen year old who did what many did under many different flags. But Averbeck's experiences are unique.

Panzerjäger: Tank Hunter begins in Chapter I: 1941, The *195. Panzerjäger Abteilung* with a brief biographical sketch, followed by an overview of Averbeck's *Panzerjäger* training. In Chapters II: 1942, Die *Hauptkampflinie*; III: 1943, An Iron Portion; and IV: 1944, The Polotsk Lowlands, personal observations reveal in great detail life and warfare on the Eastern Front, *Panzerjäger* battle tactics and equipment. Chapter V: 1944, Die *Westliche HKL*, and Chapter VI: 1945, *P.W.*, relate Averbeck's experiences on the Western Front leading to his capture. Chapter VII: Bits and Pieces recounts life as an American prisoner of war.

This work resulted from a series of personal and taped interviews conducted over a two-year period. Throughout, I have made every effort to retain the immediacy of the discourse. Few books have attempted to record the everyday life of the ordinary German soldier on the Eastern Front of World War II. It is hoped that this singular first person account will contribute to a body of knowledge that, as yet, has not reached its limit.

My thanks are extended to James L. Folkestad whose patient photographic work made more images available than I had thought possible. Additional thanks to Jurgen Averbeck without whose encouragement this story may not have been told. And finally, I extend my most heart-felt feelings to Francine, for her continued support and understanding.

CHAPTER I

1941
The 195. Panzerjäger Abteilung

I have always believed that I was born under a good star. My star must have been shining the evening my mother persuaded me to visit a doctor at the end of my second furlough from the Eastern Front. Although for nearly a year I vomited whenever I ate I had withstood her insistence that I see someone.

The doctor's diagnosis detected gastritis and upon completing the examination, he ordered me to a hospital. Over two winters on the Eastern Front I had developed the habit of breaking off small pieces of frozen, spoiled bread and sucking on them. The doctor believed that this was one of the factors contributing to my illness.

When I checked in to the hospital, the nuns placed me on a fast. Some days later I began drinking alcohol-based solutions after which they would have me swallow a catheter. But there was little need to pump my stomach. The weight of the thick rubber tube in my throat choked, then gagged me and within seconds I was throwing everything up. I was released from the hospital with ten days of recuperation furlough to recover my strength.

When I departed on my second furlough my unit, the *195. Panzerjäger Abteilung* attached to the *95. Infanterie Division*, was on the border between East Prussia and Lithuania. Fierce fighting had been going on there for more than two weeks. I was fearful that I would never see my friends again. The Russians didn't worry me, I was merely afraid of being rerouted by our own army during my return. Not being reunited with your company was the nightmare of all returning soldiers. Trainloads of eastbound soldiers from all kinds of backgrounds such as infantry, artillery, communications, engineers, tank crews, and antitank crews were often seized without warning. Everyone would be ordered off their train and used to create *Kampfengruppen* units to plug holes in a battle line. Everyone I spoke to, who went on furlough and made it back to their own unit, experienced the same fear. No one had any interest in being part of a new unit where no one knew anything about the person next to him, or performing tasks you had not been adequately trained for. Hijacking was especially common when the Russians were on the offensive as they were that summer. I left the hospital determined to find out where the 95th was fighting. To do this I had to check-in at Münster's military office.

The *Kommandantur* for Münster was furious when he found out that I had ten days of recuperation furlough.

"Soldiers on leave for ten days or less are not required to report!" he barked. Then his voice raised to a yell. "Why are you wasting my time?"

I respectfully explained that I knew I wasn't supposed to report, however, I wanted to know my unit's location.

Filled with excited expectation, I watched attentively as he grabbed his book and traced his finger over the pages. He paused, before declaring quietly, "The 95th Infantry Division is no longer in existence."

My expectations evaporated and I was suddenly aware of a vast emptiness in life as I had come to know it. All my friends I had been together with for two and a half years, through the best and the worst of times, had relied on for help and alertness to survive, had silently vanished from Germany's order of battle. I left the *Kommandantur's* office saddened and angered. I felt disoriented. My thoughts floated aimlessly. My mother's concern about my illness had saved my life but it was months before I could be thankful.

My questions, "Where will I go? What will I do?" were quickly answered. I was ordered to join a *marsch*, or replacement company at Herford, the site of my basic training in 1941, and await assignment to a new unit.

* * * * *

I was born into a Catholic family in Münster, Westphalia, on August 23, 1924.

By the early thirties the rising tension among Germans with stronger political than religious interests had degenerated into widespread attacks and harassment of the Catholic church and its organizations. In 1933, when Hitler was appointed chancellor of Germany, the Catholic hierarchy attempted to secure the freedoms of the church with a papal Concordat. Nevertheless, the harassment continued, as did Catholic protests.

The movements of the 95th Infantry Division on the Eastern Front, 1942–1944.

In 1934, when I was 10 years old, I joined the *St. Georg Pfadfindersachft*. The Catholic Scouts of Saint George was an organization similar in structure to the American Boy Scouts with uniforms of blue shirts and yellow neckerchiefs. The only difference was that we didn't go camping. I remained in the Pathfinders until 1936 when the question of how can one serve God and state simultaneously, was decided. In that year all Catholic youth organizations were dissolved and Hitler Youth (*Hitlerjugend*) membership was made compulsory for every boy 10 to 18 years of age. My friends and I were 11 and 12 years old. Although our group was an ancillary organization called the *Deutsche Jungvolk* (*DJ*), and more precisely the last rank of the *DJ* the *Pimpf*, officially we were members of the *Hitlerjugend* (HJ).

The relationship between the *Deutsche Jungvolk* and the Hitler Youth was similar to the preparatory status of Cub Scouts to Boy Scouts. We wore black pants, a brown shirt, and a black neckerchief. We were not allowed to wear the band on the left arm with the red, white, and black symbol of the National Socialist Party. Our *DJ* unit, called the *Hermann Göring Fahnlein*, contained 120 boys subdivided into three equal groups. Once a week my group assembled in a school gym. Activities during these gatherings consisted of rope knotting, song singing, studying the Nordic rune alphabet, and learning to march. When a medical unit, the *Feldscher*, was added for those boys interested in first aid, I, along with others volunteered for it. We began by attending a three-month medical course.

Our first aid instruction took place in the amphitheater for anatomy at Münster's university. We learned different bone breaks and bandaging techniques from instructors who were fourth-year medical students and young interns. I enjoyed it tremendously.

When we completed our medical training we were given an exam and those who passed received a new insignia. It was a little white patch decorated with the red rune for life and we sewed it on our left sleeve. In newspaper obituary columns the same life-rune was inverted to indicate death.

During the annual *Hitlerjugend* festivals, *Feldscher* units spread all along the parade routes and if somebody needed our help we were able to give first aid right away. We carried our supplies, including ampoules of smelling salts, in a leather pouch hung from our belt. That was always a nice duty and we enjoyed our importance.

Over school vacation *Jungvolk* members attended a big camp-out 50 miles from town. The *Feldscher* tent was marked with a red cross. While the others were playing games such as catch the flag, we took care of all the bruises and cuts associated with boys playing outside.

My training rendered me a great service in Russia where I was able to help a lot of my friends. Often during a battle our corpsmen were unable to come to the front line so you heard the wounded yelling to the left and right of you, needing help or comfort. I tried my best to make it a little easier for them and I believe that I helped quite a few men to survive—to live. I always kept up with my medical interests. I still keep my German medical books on my shelf at home.

Like all boys, on the occasion of my fourteenth birthday my enrollment in the *Jungvolk* was automatically terminated and I was inducted into the *Hitlerjugend*—at least on paper. At that time in Germany students my age either continued in school, in preparation for entering a university, or they sought out a trade school. I decided to become an electrician and for the first six months of my apprenticeship no one from the *HJ* bothered me and I didn't seek out a unit.

To tell the truth, even after I acknowledged my membership I didn't attend very often. The Hitler Youth meetings started around 7:30 or 8:00 P.M. and went until 10:00 or 10:30 P.M. Several times *HJ* representatives came to my house and asked why I didn't come more regularly to the evening meetings. I worked nine hours as an electrician's apprentice, and I didn't come home until after 5:30 P.M. And besides, when you are a teenager you have your own ideas about how to spend your time. I ran around with a bunch of guys who were also enrolled in the *HJ* and seldom, if ever, attended. This continued until one day, the *HJ* sent the police to inquire about me and so, to avoid trouble with the Party, my mother encouraged me to attend the meetings.

I went to the Hitler Youth office and asked to continue in a medical unit like that I had formerly belonged to and learned there wasn't an organization for my age group. Instead, they sent me to join a marching band. That was fine with me because I was interested in the trombone, however, when I met the band leader he said they had all the trombone players they needed. There was one position left for a brass wind instrument and they wanted a baritone.

I had joined the band late, and was weeks behind in my training. Consequently, I was told to take an instrument and study at home until I caught up. In the evenings after work, I climbed the stairs to my bedroom, took out the baritone from its case and practiced.

My bedroom was right under the roof and it had a little window that opened towards the maternity hospital where I was born. On hot summer evenings all the hospital windows were kept open. I sat beside my open window practicing with my instrument, badly, yet loudly. The music was not very melodious. My efforts ended abruptly when the head nurse visited my mother and requested I stop playing my horn "As a courtesy to the women in her hospital." I went back to the band leader and explained that I was unable to continue practicing at home. Because I was so far behind he told me to leave the unit.

In Münster some *HJ* were rowing or sailing, building sail planes or riding motorbikes. I felt that all of these were excellent alternatives to the trombone. Therefore, I could not believe it when I reported to the *HJ* office and I was assigned to a *Schar* or troop without any interesting activity. All we were doing was marching because the unit possessed nothing in the way of hobbies. This made me rebellious.

One weekend after an autumn shower, we were marching up and down a country lane when the troop leader led us right through water standing in the road. He didn't give the command to swing left or right so that we could go around the big puddle. Instead, he kept sending us stomping and splashing through the water. Each time I came to the puddle edge I jumped out and marched alongside the others until, passing the water, I rejoined the ranks. When he saw me leaving the group he blew his top, warned me to obey his commands, then marched us through the puddle again! But just as before, each time I reached the water I jumped out of line. He couldn't do anything with me except complain and I was ordered to report to the officer in charge of *Schars*, the *Gefolgschaft* leader.

I stood while the *Gefolgschaft* leader scolded me, angered that I was not respecting orders. To this charge I countered that I could not respect the leader's directives because, I blurted angrily, "What he orders is very stupid!"

With this remark he looked even more angry than before and demanded, "How dare YOU say that HE is stupid?"

"He IS stupid," I insisted. "Doesn't he know the Führer has said that we should save our shoes, and preserve our personal goods as long as possible? Our *Schar* leader is marching us through water. My boots and those of the other boys will be ruined in no time."

By quoting from the Führer there was nothing he could say against my statements or actions. He dismissed me and I never went back to the *Hitlerjugend*.

Over the next three years I devoted my energies to successfully completing my electrician's apprenticeship. Nothing distracted me until the second half of my third year of training when suddenly I had the urge to volunteer for military service. I was afraid that if I waited to be drafted there would be no war left. Besides, I think that in everyone there is a little measure of adventure and being seventeen I felt prepared to test mine. When I told my mother she emphatically refused and insisted that I wait until I was called. I couldn't join without her written agreement or that of my father who was already in the service. I relented, temporarily.

When my father came home on furlough from Poland I talked to him and together we went to the police station where he countersigned for me. I had volunteered. That evening was nearly intolerable. My mother couldn't do anything except vent her frustration which she always did very loudly. For almost two months nothing happened. Then in early November I was notified to appear at an army base near Herford, a town north of Münster, for *Panzerjäger* or antitank training.

I stayed at Herford from November to the beginning of February 1942. I was assigned a bunk in a brick barrack alongside 12 other new recruits. At Herford we learned the basics of military life, everything from marching and saluting to fire drills. Fire drill practice prepared us to assist the townsfolk in the event of an air raid. On one occasion we were placed on alert for an enemy paratroop drop. Although the night watch passed without incident, our excitement, fueled by our imaginations, kept us alert long after we were sent back to base.

The instructors at Herford introduced us to the basic procedures for artillerymen, and the care and firing of the 37 mm antitank cannon and associated equipment. At the same time, we were formally organized into *Panzerjäger* crews consisting of four men commanded by a corporal. One man became the cannoneer. He was assisted by the loader and two others whose job was the handling and the preparation of ammunition. Later two additional crewmen would carry ammunition, care for the vehicle we used to tow our cannon, or man the machine gun with which we were to protect ourselves.

By chance, I discovered I had a former school friend in another group more advanced in their training program. When we met I explained that I was terribly bored. The adventure I had been expecting was not at hand and the tedious lifestyle of a new recruit compounded the boredom. I found it aggravating to be restricted to base until we had completed our first four weeks of training. My friend told me that if I wanted to go to town I had to visit the dentist. I replied that there was nothing wrong with my teeth and he said that made no difference.

The next morning at 6:00 A.M., after our company's master sergeant finished assigning the daily tasks, he ordered anyone who was sick to go to the left. Afterwards he came by and asked each one of us what was wrong. When it came my turn I announced that I had a toothache. We had a young doctor on base and when I reported to the infirmary I learned why my friend had suggested a tooth problem. Neither our base doctor nor his staff had any dental experience. My visit was an intermediary step to freedom. Our doctor wrote a letter permitting me to go see a dentist in Herford.

I was thrilled. I hadn't even sworn the soldier's oath and I was leaving the barracks. My excitement was quickly checked. When I presented our watch commander with the letter he said, "I can't allow you out alone. You don't even have a pay book yet." Instead, he contacted a nearby company where recovering wounded soldiers were awaiting return to active duty. He assigned a lance corporal the task of accompanying me into town. I was strictly warned that any saluting was to be done by the lance corporal, not me. And, moreover, in the case of an encounter with an officer the lance corporal should say that I wasn't a soldier yet—I was only wearing the uniform.

To my relief, my guide was as excited as I was to be relieved of garrison routine. We went first to Herford's *Soldatenheim* where enlisted men could enjoy inexpensive meals, read books, play games or just listen to the radio. We ate there, had a few beers and shortly before four o'clock we went to the dentist. We were the last ones admitted to his office where I saw a sign indicating, "Closing Time 4:00 P.M." The doctor came out just long enough to greet us, look at his watch and say, "You will need to come back tomorrow." Then he signed my papers and off we went. We did this for a few more days. All the recruits in my barrack were envious. I was always out. I went to movies. I had beers. Overall, I had begun to have a great time. They on the other hand were confined to base dutifully performing and reperforming their training exercises.

On a Saturday morning in early December, at the end of our first four weeks, everyone donned what we termed our "circus uniform", due its numerous, brilliantly polished silver buttons. We were instructed to pass in review in front of our master sergeant and salute. If our demeanor and uniform passed muster we could go to town that afternoon in groups of five under our corporal's watchful eye.

When my turn came and I passed before the sergeant he yelled, "Averbeck! Get Lost!" "During the last four weeks you have spent most of your time in town and look how you are saluting all over the place!"

Nonetheless, I was allowed to leave with my roommates. I knew more about Herford than our corporal and I led them around to all the best places. We had a wonderful evening.

As time passed our knowledge about our weapon, its uses and the role of an antitank unit grew. While in training we learned that gun crews didn't have radios. The company had one, and if information needed to be sent to the various gun squads it was necessary to have infantry nearby through whom the call could be routed. Usually, we were informed, a dispatch runner or dispatch motorbike would be available. The absence of radios was a severe handicap; a shortcoming that was not apparent on the training field.

Everyone was required to check-in and check-out their paybook at the beginning and end of every leave. One Saturday afternoon I again went to town and, as was the rule before departing, I collected my paybook from my master sergeant. The movie house closed late that evening. To check in my paybook before the 10:00 P.M. curfew, I trotted through the darkness a couple of miles back to base.

I entered my barrack just as the bugle was blown. I knocked at my sergeant's door prepared to bark, "Soldier Averbeck requests permission to enter!" While at the movies I noticed that I was having difficulty swallowing. Now, no matter how hard I strained, I couldn't make a sound.

"Who is it?" came from inside.

I tried again but the best that I could manage was a strained, unintelligible wheezing.

"Who is it?" demanded the voice, more insistent and harsh than before.

Just as I realized that my ability to produce audible sound was gone the sergeant was suddenly there berating me at the top of his voice before he had fully opened his door. When at last he paused to acknowledge something was wrong he ordered me to see our doctor.

The next morning at company muster I went to the left and stood with the others going on sick call. The doctor immediately diagnosed diphtheria and had me transported to a nearby children's hospital for respiratory ailments.

I was the only soldier in a hospital full of children. They placed me in isolation and gave me two massive injections of vaccine. The first was 6,000 units and the second was 4,000 units. This was followed by a series of pills that colored my urine bright red.

I remained in isolation and all my visitors were kept on one side of a wall with a window. To further guard against the transfer of the disease the nuns ironed the letters I wrote to my mother and girlfriend.

While recovering, I was at my girlfriend's house reading the newspaper when I noticed I was having trouble with my vision. I paid it little attention even though it gradually worsened. The following week we were in a classroom studying and reciting out loud from an artillery text when it came my turn to read. I was sitting there moving the book back and forth, away and towards my eyes when the instructor asked what was the matter? I explained that I was having problems seeing the writing clearly enough to read. The next morning I again went on sick call. This time I was sent to an optometrist in Herford and a pair of eye glasses were ordered for me.

Not long thereafter we were given our regular army uniforms. On our uniforms the distinguishing signature was above our shoulders where we had a little flap piped with the color indicating our service arm. When on furlough you wore trousers with a stripe of the same color on the outside of the leg. Infantrymen wore white stripes. Engineers wore black, medical units violet, motorized units, those who brought ammunition and food from the rear, wore blue, communications wore yellow, artillerymen had red and the tank and antitank units wore pink.

In early February 1942, after what seemed like three long months we received our orders. We were being transferred to the Eastern Front. The group of young men first brought together in November were now formally known as the *1. Panzerjäger Kompanie* of the *195. Panzerjäger Abteilung*, and destined for attachment to the *95. Infanterie Division.*

I never picked up my eyeglasses. My impaired vision had resulted from the dramatic treatment I had undergone while suffering from diphtheria, and over time it became evident to me that my sight was slowly returning to normal.

We gathered our belongings and marched to the Herford railway station. From there we traveled by train to Cologne and Wahne, slowly gathering men along the way. I was unaware at the time that my parents had prepared a special going-away packet. They came to the Herford station and when they were unable to locate me, my package of food and clothing was entrusted to someone who promised to serve as an intermediary. Needless to say I never received it.

Our transport continued eastward to Berlin, Warsaw, Brest-Litovsk, Gomel, Bryansk and on to Orel on the Oka River. During the trip the winter weather became progressively colder. The warm, humid compartments lent their moisture to the frost glazing the windows. The snow, first encountered in Poland, continued along the route to Orel, our destination on the Russian steppes 240 miles south of Moscow.

Herford, Germany, 1941. Bernhard Averbeck: standing, second from left; Ludwig Kluge: standing, third from left.

Kolpny, Russia, 1942. Averbeck beside a Russian T-34 knocked out by two shots from a 3.7 cm antitank gun.

The Russian Eastern Front, spring 1942. Near the Tim and Voshnya Rivers.

Russia, Voshnya River sector, 1941–1942. Russian dead following an early morning probe of the positions of the 95th.

Russia, March 1942. Receiving provisions and mail on the Voshnya River frontline.

Russia, Voshnya River, March 1942. After receiving provisions a member of the gun crew prepares a meal.

Russia, Tim River sector, summer 1942. A sign of the 10th Artillery Company along with the Bow and Arrow, the tactical sign of the 95th Infantry Division.

Left to right: **Karl Kinschuh, unidentified, and Hermann Jahr**

Hermann Jahr

Eric Puppa, second from right, in cossack overcoat with sword.

Russia, summer 1942. Passing through the main street of a Russian village.

Russia, Tim River sector, summer 1942. Squad leaders checking area maps for the next move.

Russia, June–July 1942. Averbeck's *Spiess Oberfeldwebel* (standing) beside two cooks.

Russia, summer campaign, June 1942. A rest day behind the front line. Averbeck, foreground.

Russia, March 1942. Sun and soccer.

Russia, Tim River offensive, 1942. Antitank ammunition transports.

Russia. The 7.5 cm antitank gun on which Averbeck was riding, destroyed by a mine during the summer campaign of 1942.

CHAPTER II

1942
Die Hauptkampflinie

PANZERJÄGER units were mechanized troops but when we arrived at Orel neither our guns nor our trucks were at hand so we set off on foot to Kolpny, 60 miles to the south, and from there to the village of Gustaya about five miles behind the front line. Each of us carried two sacks of our personal belongings. To make the walking a little easier we passed our waist belts through the grips of the sacks and swung them from our shoulders. When we chanced upon a shipment of sleds we helped ourselves. The sleds made the traveling much less difficult. Still, we seldom made more than ten miles a day in the snow and soon a long, grey line stretched over the march route. I struggled to keep up, but I found myself easily exhausted and short of breath, a result of my recent bout with diphtheria. At the end of each day I was often the last to arrive. Our march took ten days with one or two rest days in-between. We arrived at Gustaya on February 20 and rested there for about a week.

Two weeks before we joined the company, between the 4th and the 18th of February 1942, the 95th Infantry Division was attacked in the vicinity of the Voshnya and Tim Rivers. At that time our antitank company possessed Dunkurque surplus, 4-wheel drive English Bedfords that were well suited to pulling our 37 mm antitank gun. After the February Russian offensive, the division counter-attacked and retook their old positions. Unfortunately, many of the English transports were lost during this time.

Bedfords were commonly abandoned due to dirty gasoline or frozen gas lines. There was a little in-line filter in a glass container that you could unscrew and clean out. In temperatures ranging from 20 to 40 degrees below zero your fingers stiffen and it becomes difficult to manipulate small objects. If fumbling cold-numbed fingers dropped the glass bulb onto a metal part of the engine and it broke, the truck was worthless. We were without replacement parts. When the 195th was forced to retreat they lost a lot of guns and the Bedfords that pulled them. That was where the dead ones came in.

The day before our arrival the Russians had re-attacked division positions at Kolpny and killed four men. They had just brought the dead from the front line to headquarters at Gustaya for burial when we arrived. Our first introduction to death came when we prepared their graves. We dug depressions in the deep snow and erected four crosses of a uniform design to mark their location. With the arrival of spring some other group would be assigned the task of placing the bodies in the soil.

From Gustaya we continued on to our ultimate destination the *Hauptkampflinie* or front line, known by its acronym *HKL* to those of us who were there.

On our arrival we were directed to find ourselves places in a wooden hut filled with veterans gathered in small groups talking or playing cards. I entered the doorway and after my eyes had adjusted to the gloom, I saw that the furniture was limited to a large brick stove, a table with chairs, and blanket-covered straw for sleeping. Just in front of me a soldier eating at the table was silently watching the man in the chair beside him picking off body lice then triumphantly crushing each new discovery on the table top with his thumbnail.

Overnight, lice invaded our clothing and bodies and they were impossible to eradicate. Outside you were cool enough so that they were not too active. But during the night when you were lying on the straw amid others who were already snoring, your body warmed and the bugs began crawling about, and you could scratch yourself until you were bloody. Either you were outside shivering in 40 degree below zero temperatures or inside and warm with the lice biting you. This lasted until March or April, depending on the weather, because after that we were sleeping outdoors. When we moved outside we thought that our pest problem had been solved until we discovered that during the summer months fleas were a regular nuisance. These may have been some sort of sand flea because they never bothered us during the winter. Flies were also bothersome as were the mosquitoes. Everyday we swallowed a little yellow pill of antiprene to protect us from malaria.

Tactical symbols identified the various units operating in our division's zone. Tactical symbols were painted on road signs and the sides of vehicles. Our symbol was the bow and arrow, and it was neatly painted throughout our area.

My company, the 195th, was a special self-sustaining antitank unit attached to the *95. Infanterie Division*. The 95th had been formed in 1939 from reservists of the 6th *Wehrkreis* military district that encompassed Münster. The division had participated in the invasion of France and the taking of Kiev. In the German army of that period a division consisted of three regiments. Each regiment had three battalions and each battalion had twelve companies. The antitank force was the thirteenth company.

Antitank companies were responsible for guarding regimental areas against enemy tank attack. The 195th operated division wide and could be thrown in whenever a regiment's thirteenth company could not halt an enemy's tank attack. In effect, the 195th became the 95th's "thirteenth company."

Our *HKL* position was on an open plain. The Russian line was in a forest a scant 300 to 400 yards to the east. We dug our guns in so that the barrels rested just above the hard-crusted snow and we spent considerable time trying to camouflage them.

At that time our gun was the 37 mm, and it was less than affectionately called an *Einklopfkanone*—a door knocker cannon.

During the Russian assault on our positions at Kolpny just prior to our arrival, the antitank crews had come under attack by Russian T-34 tanks. One gun crew waited until a tank was within point-blank range then fired their first round. The shell exploded against the driver's spring-loaded hatch causing it to pop open. A quickly fired second round went through the open hatch and destroyed the tank from the inside out. It had been an episode of unprecedented good luck because the 37 mm was unable to penetrate the frontal armor of any Soviet tank, hence the term "door knocker." This imbalance of power was redressed somewhat when we received 50 mm cannons. We brought the first 50 up to the front line on a horse-pulled sled.

We did possess special grenade-like projectiles for 37 mm cannons. Upon contact these shells burned their way through a tank's armor. Launched with a simple powder charge, four little fins stabilized its flight. Its range was about 100 to 150 yards. There was a great reluctance to use them because in order to put it in the barrel you had to move out from behind the protection of the gun shield. With Russian infantry charging in front, exposing yourself during loading was inviting immediate death.

I soon learned that winter on the Russian front was a time to consolidate lines and bring up supplies and replacements like ourselves. Winter controlled the front and for the most part we and our enemy, begrudging its presence, waited out its temporary dominion.

From the end of February to May nothing big was happening. In fact, life was so uneventful that those of us who were new in the hut would run outside with the first sound of gunfire. That was how innocent we were.

For the most part life on the *HKL* revolved around guard duty where we soon learned that the Russians were very good at camouflage.

You don't always know the topography of the land facing your front line position. You have a certain sector to watch and you did this with the utmost care. Sometimes, maybe a mile away you would see a Russian soldier and while you were observing him he would vanish. Then after a while you would see him again. At first we thought it was the same Russian. However, during the day we probably saw 20 to 30 soldiers appear and disappear.

When it started getting towards dusk, when it was no longer quite light and not yet dark, all of a sudden 30 enemy soldiers rose up in front of you screaming OORAY! as they charged your gun from 100 yards. Believe me, we were surprised.

From the outset we learned to watch our area carefully and observe everything. Usually, even when we were on night guard duty, we had two guys on the gun in case it was necessary to shoot. One man loaded, and one corrected the firing. We kept ourselves alert because the Russians were also adept in reconnaissance.

We didn't have white camouflage uniforms during the winter of 1941–1942. The Russians, on the other hand, wore white and traveled on skis. They had often overpowered and killed our guards with knives and disappeared before anyone knew what had happened. Sometimes they would take a captive for interrogation.

On my gun there were two of us from Herford, and both of us were 18 years old whereas the rest of the men were in their 30s. Some were even older. We had a different spirit—we were always ready to go. The others were just hoping to make it through the day with a minimum of effort.

To relieve the late winter tedium, I volunteered for night reconnaissance on two occasions. Normally reconnaissance was done by the infantry. They were thrilled whenever one of us would volunteer because it meant fewer of them would have to go.

A first sergeant always accompanied us. We wore our helmets and carried our rifle and bayonets. There was always some anxious joking when we would leave, more for bravado than humor. We would meet some infantry first sergeant in the trenches in front of our position. Then, using our trenches, we would move as close as we could before crawling over the top. We had to maneuver on stomachs past mined obstacles and uncollected dead until we could sneak through the Russian line and into their rear. On both occasions we were to observe and report back whatever we felt was most noteworthy. One night we snuck into the back of a village. Each time we heard something we went slowly and silently in the opposite direction.

Our vehicles never had heaters and so the drivers delivering ammo and food, who were sometimes driving hundreds of miles, were issued heavy overcoats that went down to their ankles. Whenever I was on guard duty I wore my regular uniform plus a big driver's overcoat I had been lent. With all this clothing I had to force the strap of my rifle over the padding on my shoulder. It was very clumsy and the rifle stuck so tightly in place that whenever I needed it I had to ask someone to pull it off.

Without white winter uniforms our movements were easily detected even when our gun was well camouflaged. We soon resorted to recovering winter pants, jackets, and felt boots from the Soviet dead. We did this without any real forethought as to the possible dangers until one day a "dead" Russian killed one of our men. Afterwards we always carried our rifles and from 50 yards made sure that the dead were indeed dead before venturing closer.

I later discovered that when an attack was faltering the enemy soldiers in the vanguard would drop onto the snow and play dead. When it was close to nightfall I would watch the "dead" stand up here and there and walk the other way. They had been lying there the whole day in below zero temperatures. That was testimony to the quality of their winter gear.

That first winter there was a lot of improvisation as far as weapons and personal equipment was concerned. Neither our men nor our vehicles were prepared for the harshness of the winter, and so we made do with what we had and supplanted this with ingenuity and resourcefulness.

In the winter evenings we always found some wood and parked the trucks on top of it so that they were not resting in the snow or ice, and later the mud. Everything froze solid during the night and the next morning the ground was like cement. When our tracked vehicles froze in place we used gasoline to set the ground afire so that it would soften enough for us to drive away.

Gun leaders carried a pistol and a machine pistol, all the rest of us had rifles. The machine pistol that was issued during the winter of 1941–1942 was one of our most personally dangerous weapons. One night our corporal came off duty, and as was his habit, took his machine pistol and hung it from a peg on the wall.

Somehow the peg gave way and the pistol fell to the floor letting go four to five rounds right into him, killing him outright. There was no way to securely lock the safety on it. This must have been a frequent occurrence because not too long thereafter everyone with this weapon was issued a little leather strap. The strap kept the safety lever secure so that if the pistol was jarred it would not automatically begin firing. In the next six months we received new models of the same machine pistol equipped with a handle that you had to pull back and a trigger lock. Nevertheless, just as with the leather strap, these safety devices were not always certain. This pistol was reissued with a better safety but for our corporal and for quite a few other men it came too late.

Aside from the lack of specialized winter gear our supply was very good. Our *Spiess Oberfeldwebel* or as we called him "the mother of the company" always made sure that front line gun crews were served a hot meal everyday. Men from the kitchen came from the rear carrying the food in special cannisters on their backs. This was not easy because they often came under fire. Besides our army rations the *Spiess* always tried to supplement our food by buying fresh meat, or getting surplus flour to make extra bread. A company was always in readiness if it had a good "mother" looking after the men.

Eric Puppa spoke perfect Russian and served as our interpreter. He played the guitar and accompanied his playing with his terrific tenor voice. He also liked to talk. When Eric was talking you could leave for guard duty and when you returned two hours later he would still be going strong.

Fraternization was strictly forbidden. Nonetheless, Eric Puppa, a native of East Prussia, always had his eye on a woman. On two occasions the resulting encounters required that he seek medical attention for gonorrhea. This was a serious offense punishable with seven days of jail time. Problems requiring medical attention were noted in your paybook as a number and letter code. To avoid punishment Eric would alter the number written in his book. For example, if 36C were the code for a venereal disease visit, he would change it to read 38C.

Eric was a natural entertainer and he liked magic. When supplies of fresh goods were low, he would help our *Spiess* make ends meet by entertaining the farmers in the nearest village. In the morning he would walk around the village center producing a card out of thin air or a coin from behind someone's ear. While performing, he would announce that there would be a magic show and folk music that evening. The entrance charge might be two fresh eggs for each adult. Offers to buy food were often ignored or met with resistance, but Eric's singing and magic never failed to win over the children and their parents. He often returned with enough fresh goods for the entire company.

In the course of my first winter, the crew on one of our neighboring guns was inside their hut playing cards when the door opened. Nobody paid any attention. Even if they had, they would not have made any remark because anyone with all his winter clothing on looked just like anyone else. The man entered unchallenged, closed the door, stood his rifle in the corner, and went over to the fire.

When the card players looked up momentarily they were astonished to see a Russian soldier. He was standing there clapping and rubbing his hands together and repeating "cold" in Russian, rather than the German *kalt, kalt*.

He stood beside the brick oven warming himself and not moving. One of the men snuck around behind him and took away his rifle. The visitor divulged to a crewmen who spoke Russian, that he was tired of the war and that for him the war was over.

That gun crew kept him for about four weeks. Everyday he drew and carried the water, split wood, and kept the fire going. In the night he slept amongst the others in that hut. In the spring, when various groups were leaving in preparation for the upcoming summer offensive, they brought him to our company and he stayed with us for a while longer. The sergeant removed all the identifying emblems from one of our old jackets and gave it to him. He formally surrendered when we departed.

March brought the first hints of spring thaw and longer sun-filled days that encouraged the water dripping from roofs and tree branches. As the snow cover shrank, pathways of dirty hard-packed ice became treacherous, glistening, puddle-filled raceways. Warm, spring breezes accelerated the thaw. Soon the snow was a memory, its principal souvenir the watery surpluses permeating the earth's surface.

The characteristics of spring travel and combat were always the worse kind. The roads were like molasses and you were up to your knees in mud. Horses were the easiest means of transport. However, with our half-tracks we really didn't have as hard a time as vehicles with tires. We helped lots of cars by giving them a push or pulling them from mud holes using our tow cables.

That spring we and our clothing were cleaned at a *Delausung* in a village in the rear. The *Delausung* consisted of an extremely hot steam treatment and signs were posted everywhere warning that ammunition left in pockets could blow up. Afterwards we were free of lice until winter when we moved indoors again.

One day, while still on the Voshnyna tributary to the Tim River, I was dispatched from the *HKL* to company headquarters some four miles behind our front lines. The river course had cut deeply into the ground there and, in some areas, was separated by high banks. I was on foot, walking along the road when my attention was caught by our *Fiesler Storch* flying overhead. The *Fiesler Storch* was a slow-flying, two-seater airplane used by the division commander. We would often see it flying over the front line.

I was watching our airplane when two Russian fighters appeared on the horizon flying quickly towards the slower craft. I still remember seeing the red star and letters preceding a series of numbers painted on their fuselages. As soon as the fighters turned into the path of our *Storch* the pilot increased his speed. The Russians quickly closed the gap and just as they came within striking range the *Storch* stalled and dropped 50 to 60 feet. The two fighters swept past him without firing a shot. Our pilot kept his plane in the shadows of the gorge while the Russians flew across the river a couple of times. Unable to find where he had secreted himself, they gave up and flew away to the east. Soon our *Storch* re-emerged and continued it journey.

My first combat came in the spring of 1942 after we had departed Gustaya, our home for the last three months. In May the whole division participated in a new offensive against the Russians that began at the end of the month and continued through to the beginning of June.

On our way we bivouacked in an apple orchard and it was there that we received instruction in the 75 mm antitank gun and how to fire mixed ammunition. Anyone being fired on by regular artillery rounds had a 50/50 chance of survival, if they hit the dirt. We were issued antitank shells tipped in steel and regular high explosive (HE), antipersonnel rounds. On the head of every HE projectile there was a screw-activated delayed fuse. With the screw turned in, or out, the HE projectile hit the ground and deflected into the air, spraying its blast downwards and forwards rather than expending its force upwards.

To tow the 75 we received half-ton half-tracks. At this time others were still driving a few old Austin transports left over from the 1941–1942 winter action. Our company officers had American 4-door Fords. The rest of our vehicles were German trucks and cars.

In preparation for the summer campaign our division was assigned to straighten out a small area of the front line in the region of the Voronezh River; that was our objective.

When I first arrived in Gustaya individual assignments were handed out to everyone except myself and for a while I lacked an appointment to a particular gun crew. Instead, I moved from one gun to the next and helped where I could. This was fine when we were holding our static positions at Gustaya. But while preparing for the offensive I soon tired of walking so when one of our vehicles towing a cannon came alongside I hitched a ride on the spars that served to pull the gun. When I got on a crewman assigned to that gun, who was doing the same thing, turned towards me and said, "You better get off or I'll kick your ass!" I took one look at him, thrust my lower jaw forward and countered, "Kiss mine!" I quickly jumped up to escape the blows that I was sure were coming next. I had reached the half-track when all of a sudden there was a loud Boom! I looked back and there was the gun lying upside down in a cloud of dust. The truck had driven over a mine and the gun had taken the explosion. The cannon was ruined yet my antagonist was unharmed. He was angry because he hadn't even received as much as a scratch. "If I had at least broken an arm or leg I could have gone home," he said angrily. It was the first gun we lost in the offensive.

On the day of the attack we entered a staging area to await our turn to move forward. When we were called up we draped flags over the hoods of our vehicles to identify us to the Stuka pilots passing overhead. Near the battle area tall pencil-shaped dark clouds, the explosions of our airstrikes, could be seen rising from the horizon line. Nearer still, two lines of uniformed cyclists were pedaling into the distance.

When we started out in 1942, the *195. Panzerjäger Abteilung* consisted of four companies, two were antitank companies and two were companies on bicycles. It is a funny thing when you are going forward in an offensive and all of a sudden you see a whole company of soldiers riding on bicycles towards the battle. They had retained the traditions of the cavalry but instead of horses they had bicycles. By given order they would stop, put their bicycles together, and advance farther on foot, leaving just one or two guys behind. I observed this a couple of times. Later in the war these two units were given to the infantry so that afterwards our company consisted of two heavy antitank companies. Bicycle companies were ultimately suspended.

Prior to our reorganization, two young men of about my age were transferred to a bicycle company. They were easy going country boys, always looking for a good time and, therefore, seemingly always in trouble. I'm sure our officers felt that they were ridding themselves of two characters who were without any possible worth. The paradox was that the younger of the two really distinguished himself. At the height of the battle he collected a basket full of our egg-shaped grenades and sprinted across into the Russian lines. Then he walked along dropping the grenades into one foxhole after the other.

It was a slow process to activate a grenade. Each grenade had a cap that had to be unscrewed allowing a cord with a small porcelain pearl on the end to drop out. To activate the explosive you had to grasp the pearl, jerk on the cord and count 21, 22, 23 before releasing it. Although there was plenty of time for him to be hurt nothing happened. He broke the Russian line and received the Iron Cross first and second class for his bravery.

When we got to the front we were directed to set up our gun in a farmyard and repel any Russian counterattack. We unhooked our gun from the half-track and rolled it into a log stable right on the battle line. To sight it, we found that it was necessary to remove two logs. We didn't have long to wait. While setting up, Russian tanks appeared.

As was our practice we loaded our gun, and with more ammo ready, held our fire until the Russian tanks were well within range. With our first shot we thought we had been targeted. The force of the muzzle blast expending itself inside the small enclosure stung our ears, collapsed the remaining logs above the barrel, and choked us with a cloud of powder-fine dust. We were in the path of the oncoming assault. With logs lying in a jumbled mass around our gun, and visually blinded by the cloud of dust filling the air, we were unable to return fire. We grabbed our rifles and prepared to defend the stable. The Russians continued to advance until they were mixing with our own troops and tanks. We were watching the melee through the cracks between the logs when one of our Stukas dropped its bomb in the farmyard and with a deafening explosion the air refilled with dust. Blinded and deafened for a second time, we waited anxiously until our sight cleared when we were relieved to discover that the battle had shifted to our left.

During this, our first major battle, we knocked out six T-34s, lost two guns to direct fire, and had numerous wounded including my platoon leader. Near where I was a gun knocked out a T-34 150 to 200 yards in front of their position. Two Soviet crewmen emerged from the wreck and stood beside their tank. I watched as a dispatcher drove out on a motorcycle with his platoon leader in the side car to take the two prisoner.

As they neared, one of the Russian tankers killed the platoon leader with a single shot to the head then dropped his weapon and put up his hands. Without a given command everyone from that gun picked up his rifle and fired. I saw the body of the Soviet tanker lift as it violently sprawled backwards.

In the course of our offensive on the Voshnya tributary to the Tim River we encountered a small river over which our engineers later built a bridge. Before it was ready, two infantry regiments of the 95th forded the river. We were left behind in reserve with the remaining regiment until the bridge was open for traffic.

The attack was to formally begin after the initial force crossed the river. We watched until they disappeared over a distant ridge. A few minutes had gone by when without any warning rockets began passing overhead with a loud YEUUW—YEUUW—YEUUW sound. The regiments on the other side of the river panicked. They turned around, not knowing what was the source of the noise, and prepared to recross the river. When we first heard the noise and saw the smoke trails overhead we were ready to go with them. Before we could act, some officers arrived, calmed everyone down, and explained that six six-barreled multiple-rocket launching *Nebelwerfer* guns were firing a preassault barrage. This was a new weapon and experience for us.

When we advanced we saw the Russian dead. There wasn't a mark on them. It was explained to us that exploding 110 mm *Nebelwerfer* rockets created a vacuum, suffocating anyone within range. We heard that the Russians complained about them and warned that they were going to use gas. This only gave us something else to worry about. The Russian Katushyas exploded like regular artillery and with them I never experienced anything like the effect of the *Nebelwerfers*.

We continued fighting for another four to five days until reaching our designated destination, we stopped.

Enemy snipers haunted the front line. Russian sharpshooters carried a fully automatic ten-shot rifle with a scope. They were good with their rifles and we learned from them what we could and couldn't do. Usually one mistake was all that was allowed; *appropriate* behavior became second nature.

I was relaxing on a brick wall, enjoying the rays of a sun that contained the promise of a warm summer. The "PHHHT" sound that threw up red brick dust sent me tumbling for cover. The sniper's bullet had passed between my legs and buried itself in the bricks. My white winter trousers had made a fine target. A little higher and the rifleman could have ended my thoughts of ever raising a family and higher still he could have ended my thoughts altogether.

When talking amongst ourselves some would say, "I have a feeling I will get killed." One fellow named Karl Kinschuh, who had been wounded and returned to the company on the same day that we arrived, repeatedly said he wouldn't make it home again and sure enough within two to three months he was dead. We buried Karl in a cemetery beside a Russian orthodox church.

My own death never entered my mind. I always found this sort of talk pretty strange because I can honestly say that in all my experiences in both theaters I never had the feeling I wouldn't make it. I was not considered happy-go-lucky nor was I reckless. I just somehow knew what I had to do to survive and that is something no one can teach you. Certainly, someone can instruct you on how to conduct yourself under fire and so on. However in combat, no one can give you a program and say, "Hey listen, if it happens like this do this or that." For the most part, when in battle my instinct took over. If somebody asked me later on, "How come you did it this way?" I would say, "I don't know." I always acted accordingly to the situation.

Churches, like that where we buried Karl, dotted the countryside and although our chaplains put them to use, most had been long boarded up, converted into stables, or municipal storage space. The following spring I had the opportunity to visit the cathedral of Smolensk. In the darkened interior smoke from innumerable votive candles hung in an air heavily scented with incense. The tiny candles were like yellow-orange eyes blinking at the people silently arriving to initiate another bright-eyed gaze. I spent one hour in undisturbed tranquility: nothing else existed.

When moving into firing position, we unhooked our gun from the half-track, unloaded boxes of shells along with the ammo belts for our machine gun, and grabbed our rifles. Then our driver drove the half-track to a secure location from where we could see him and he us. When we ran low on ammo we would signal the driver to return by holding an empty ammunition box or shell in a horizontal position above our head.

On several occasions this routine was abruptly interrupted as, when on one afternoon two T-34s immediately fired on us. A railroad embankment separated us from the Russian tanks parked about 600 to 700 yards distant. When we arrived, instead of our gun leader kneeling down and looking to be sure that we could clear the crown of the embankment, he had simply indicated where to place the gun. When we came under fire, our gunner looked through the cannon's sight to determine the range and swore saying, "I can't shoot. We have half the hill in the gun sight." When the driver saw our signal he came back to help us. We hooked the gun to the half-track and made a circle, dragging it around to a new position facing the T-34s. We stopped less than 100 yards from the embankment where a depression of about two feet allowed us to shoot. Just then our new 1st lieutenant, who was also the company leader, arrived in his open-topped, 4 wheel-drive *Kommandowagen*. He threw open one of the swing doors and demanded to know why were we not shooting? Our squad leader explained that the gun had been too low and we needed to relocate it onto higher ground. He then turned and ordered me to go to the embankment and give fire coordinates. With an antitank gun you always need to have someone observing out front because with each round fired, the barrel blast sent dust and everything flying up. In such instances you are unable to see if you hit the target, or the ground in front, to the side or in the back of a tank. My job was to correct the fire and give new coordinates using arm and hand signals. I ran over to the berm, clambered up to the edge and from there began directing fire towards the T-34s.

Whenever we were uncertain of the distance we fired three shots. The first shot was to the estimated range, for example 600 yards, and discovering that it was 50 yards too short you would add another 50 yards. If you were lucky you got a hit, if not, and you struck behind the tank, you could correct your aim for a third time which generally placed you on target.

The Russians saw all the activity we were engaged in and kept us under constant fire. Luckily for our gun crew, the tankers shooting at us were lousy gunners. Each time they were firing it was either too long or too short. Then suddenly, as the driver was moving out of range, they struck our half-track on the back just above the fenders where we had special racks to hold our *Tellerminen* or T-mines. *Tellerminen* were so named because of their flatness resembling a dinner plate. Fortunately nothing happened although large shrapnel cut right through some of the mines. There was no explosion because they were useless without their primers in them. If by some freak accident they had ignited, the driver and vehicle would have disappeared. The accident turned out to have a practical side. We later built a sturdy storage box over the back of our half-track where it had been damaged.

The two tanks were sitting side by side, at most 30 yards apart, still shooting at us without effect. With our second shot I had the exact distance and we knocked them both out, one after the other.

We had good leaders and usually the ones who were, were young men. Because the 195th was originally a reserve unit we had a wide range of ages. The average age was 35 years plus. Those of us who were 18 years old were really babies compared to the old timers. Whenever we had action we were always anxious to go whereas the older ones were more cautious and thoughtful.

Despite our readiness to engage the enemy none of the young men I arrived with from Herford were ever lost in combat during any time that I was with them. On the front line we always received harassing fire and that was when we had a couple of fellows wounded and one killed. With very few exceptions the relief group of February 1942, of which I was a part, were all together until the time that I went on my second furlough in May of 1944.

When the infantry wasn't there a couple of us younger ones would go up front with our rifles to keep the enemy at bay. We were always lucky that no one was hit while we were doing it.

One time our gun was in an open field with numerous small depressions. A Russian machine gun squad advanced to a nearby depression and placed us under fire. To allow ourselves time to organize return fire, four of us countercharged the new Russian position. If we hadn't done something we would have been overrun.

It is a peculiar feeling when you hear the machine gun shooting from the Russian side and on the ground you see the shots coming closer and closer. We ran towards the little fountains of soil spraying into the air until in a split second we broke left and right and took cover, making ourselves as small as possible on the ground. Nobody was hit. We all got up and advanced farther, and the same thing happened. The Russian machine gunner directed his fire to us, shooting low and raising it slowly to find us, his targets, before we dropped. Again nobody was hurt.

It was at that moment that I put my head up and found the machine gun. I raised up on one knee, aimed and fired, taking the machine gunner out of action. Although we were only about 100 yards away, we were not permitted to follow through and get into the Russian positions. Our corporal called us back to our gun emplacement.

None of the older guys would ever come along with us. They were really cautious because most were married and had children. Today I can understand their point of view. When I was 18 and 19 years old I was a free spirit in that respect. Nonetheless, their conservative approach could be angering as on several occasions when our gun leader lacked the guts to take the initiative and start shooting. When, "Shoot only to defend yourself" orders were issued they were often a big mistake. We didn't have radio communication with our company headquarters so we always had to dispatch someone to ask permission to commence firing. By the time a runner returned the situation had oftentimes changed.

After several more intensive engagements we were pulled out of the front line for a 24-hour rest. We arrived at our destination during the night and used our rain shelters to make a tent. An artillery group with four 210 mm field guns appeared and set up on a low hilltop barely 30 yards away from us. Exhausted, we quickly fell asleep.

At 5:00 A.M. the next morning we heard some talking nearby but didn't pay it any attention until all four guns started firing. The noise and force of the shock waves buffeted our tents, rudely jerking us from our rest, wide-eyed and deafened.

We were held strictly responsible for all our gear. We had a standing order requiring that you always kept your gas mask on your person. Anyone caught by an officer on the roads without their gas mask could get three days lockup. The infantry carried their gas masks all of the time. Because we were motorized we kept our masks on the trucks. This was against the standing order. When we would set up, we detached our gun, unloaded our ammunition and the rest of the necessary equipment and then our driver departed to a safe distance taking our gas masks with him. We gave little serious thought about our habit until that fall.

Every night the Russians flew over us with a biplane we nicknamed the *Nahmaschine* because the motor resembled the roh-roh-roh-roh of an old sewing machine. It was a little two seater, and they were never flying very high, so sometimes when we had a full moon we would shoot tracers at it.

They would use a loudspeaker to call down telling us we should surrender and that we would have a wonderful life with lots of food. Other times they would drop artillery ammunition that never exploded. These rounds needed to reach a certain velocity in order to explode and this was impossible from such low heights. We always had a good laugh when they were flying around us. We had heard that plane so many evenings that we were conditioned to accept it as a nuisance.

One night the *Nahmaschine* was in our vicinity again and someone from our gun who was on guard duty was yelling Gas! Gas! Gas! Our eyes widened when to the horror of everyone a knee-high, dense veil crossed the ground and passed us. We really panicked because our truck was at least 300 to 400 yards behind us and no one could have reached it and their mask before succumbing to the gas. To our relief the opaque cloud was an evening fog.

We very seldom experienced fog in the late summertime but the area was not a flat plain. There were little gullies and heights and it was in one of the little ditches that the fog formed and rolled out in our direction. The experience had an impact.

For the next several weeks we always had our gas masks at hand. We could never substantiate the rumor claiming that the Russians had yellow gas for their front line grenade launchers and that reserves of this gas had been discovered by one of our reconnaissance groups, but we had a sudden appreciation for its potential validity.

That same fall the need for radios among the gun crews and clean weaponry was driven home to me. Our machine gun was the MG34 and it was very efficient when it was operating properly. To ensure that it would fire correctly you had to keep it exceptionally clean because it was sensitive to the smallest amounts of dirt. We even tied rags where the belt feeder was so that dust or grime didn't enter by there. A machine gun with a fouled mechanism would send 1-2-3 shots and then stop working. At such times you had to manually pull back the mechanism to fire, and pull it back again. and again until it operated freely. Sometimes that would clear it; if not you were in deep trouble.

During that first autumn a wild honeybee hive was discovered near our position. A fellow in our company, who was a farmer in civilian life and had experience with bees, recovered the honeycomb. On the next ration distribution day every crew received some of the hive. We kept ours in a pot on our half-track.

A few days later a Russian infantry force numbering about twenty-five men attacked us. Their advance escaped our attention until they suddenly rose up and charged forward. Their commissar stayed in the back like a shepherd, haranguing his men forward with yells and shots from his machine pistol.

There were bushes around us so we had a little cover but the attack was coming at an angle to our gun position. We had maybe 15 degrees to the left and right and it was inadequate leeway to bring fire onto the enemy troops. We had to swing our gun around.

After a couple of shots were fired from a gun the spades forming the end of the spars dug deep into the ground and ours were well set. This made it hard to move any large caliber gun on the spur of the moment. First, it was necessary to roll the gun forward and then try to lift the back prior to swinging it around. We tried once, pushing against the wheels, but failed to dislodge the spades. To our shock as we were about to try a second time the gun crew to our left and rear rolled their gun from its position, attached it to their half-track and departed. They had a clear view of us and the approaching Russians and would have been able to give us cover with high-explosive rounds. Instead they packed up everything and left.

We attempted to move the gun two more times and on the last try we succeeded, due I believe more to fear than to strength. We brought the spars together, rolled the gun forward and fixed it to the half-track. Russian bullets were hitting to the right and the left of us, and ricocheting off the gun and half-track—after which everyone instinctively ducked—but we went unscathed.

We pulled back and gained the distance necessary to go into position when something went wrong and we were unable to fire the gun. Our cannoneer checked the firing mechanism while we returned fire with our rifles. We managed to wound a few of the slowly approaching Russians when, to make matters worse, our MG34 jammed. Our machine gunner kept pulling back on the handle and he would send off two or three rounds before it would jam again. No matter how quickly he worked the mechanism the situation was getting worse. When one of the Russian bullets killed our driver we decided to withdraw.

Our corporal unscrewed the cap of a stick grenade and the little pearl of porcelain attached to its cord dropped out. He jerked on the cord, counted 21, 22, 23, and then slid it into the barrel. The blast destroyed the firing mechanism from the inside. By this time the Russians were so close I could see every detail of their faces. We began withdrawing through the bushes, stopping occasionally to fire our rifles. When they got to the half-track they were distracted enough to temporarily forget about us and we were able to break off. We walked two miles back to our unit's headquarters where we made a plan to recover our half-track and our dead comrade.

Because of our escape we were familiar with the terrain and sneaking back we found that the Russians were still with our vehicle and enjoying the honey. We only fired a few shots before they all surrendered to our calls of, "*Ruki Verch*!" Hands Up!

The Russian soldiers that first year were good fighters especially when you had elite troops in front of you such as the Stalin Guard. In combat you could really feel the difference if they were elite troops or soldiers 35 years or over who didn't have the staying power of the younger ones.

We always searched the Russian prisoners we captured. Generally, each one carried a little canvas haversack of poor manufacture closed by draw strings. They usually had something they called *kascha*, a grain-like porridge, dried fish and blackbread. They had no containers for tea or water. In comparison, I'm sure that our monthly ration of a half bottle of cognac and 200 cigarettes was a luxury unknown to most of them.

Our friend's death had been unnecessary. A radio would have allowed us to coordinate our activity with the gun crew that had deserted us, or with nearby infantry. Without radios we were frequently in the dark as to whether a defensive line still existed. Many times when the infantry was supposed to be 200 yards in front of us our gun would suddenly be confronted by a Russian breakthrough. Sometimes we were able to repel the assault, sometimes not. We subsequently learned that the infantry were purposely breaking to the right and left of the Russian attack and then closing ranks after their passage. Radios would have allowed us to organize our activities to the benefit of everyone concerned.

After the honey incident, we were temporarily without a gun so our crew was reassigned. For a while I became a dispatcher and observer.

When we encountered Russian tanks their tactics were often not very good. Our Panzers generally operated so that there was one tank in the front and one in the back to give fire protection. And, our tanks were always in contact with their radios. In this way, if a tank commander saw a Russian antitank gun he could give its location to the nearest Panzers which would bring it under fire. The Russians didn't have radios in their tanks and in the beginning of the war they suffered heavy losses. Our tank and antitank positions were not easily detected and even when they were, there was no way for the Russians to communicate this between tanks. I presume that the American Grant and Sherman tanks we encountered were also without radios.

Without radios, the tanks next to the one that we were shooting at didn't know their companion was being targeted, until we got a hit. Nonetheless, the neighboring tanks had no idea where we were with our gun.

Our division's intelligence was always listening in on the Russian radio frequencies and the Russians sometimes communicated in uncoded, clear text. In those instances we knew exactly where the next Russian advance would be and, in accordance with their radio calls, we organized the necessary defense in that area.

While working as an observer I had the opportunity to see one of our prepared responses in operation. I sat in the gable of a house with a pair of powerful field glasses made like twin periscopes referred to as a *Shere*. Through the *Shere* I had a good view of the battlefield. About 3,000 yards from us the Russian tanks emerged from the fringe of a forest where they had been camouflaged and stopped on the edge of an open plain in one long continuous line. Their commander was in a small T60 tank equipped with a 20 mm cannon. I watched as he stood in his turret and drove from one tank to the next. The tank commanders of each successive tank were standing in their turrets. The T60 would stop, the commander would issue his orders, and drive on to the next crew. When the T60 had moved on, the previous commander would go down inside his tank and all the hatches were closed. Only after the commander had spoken with everyone did his tanks start advancing towards us.

The first line consisted of all T-34s, behind were several Kaleshki Valenki Is and IIs. The KVI was a 44-ton tank with a 76.2 mm main gun. The KVII was a giant of over 50 tons with a 122 mm gun mounted in a square turret. These tanks always stayed behind the smaller, quicker T-34s and destroyed any resistance to the lighter armor.

As they advanced across the rough ground the Russian tanks gathered speed and pretty soon their main guns were jerking all about. Their lack of precision while firing on the move was an indescribable gift to us. Our tanks broke cover and moved out, stopped at positions affording the best protection, fired on a target, and moved on. In a brief and furious exchange the Soviet armored attack was crushed.

When we were near the end of our offensive, the Russians turned on their propaganda loudspeakers. "Come over here," they would call in German. "We have lots of women and food, just bring your mess kit." These broadcasts were followed by recordings of German marches. One night they called to us saying that the 95th would be leaving soon, and not to worry, because they would get us anyhow. And sure enough in a couple of days we were transferred out of there. For a while, we didn't see much action as we traveled north behind the front line.

The Russians were a poor people. In the small rural villages there were few cement or brick homes, everything was built of wood. Typically, ninety percent of the interior was one room with a *prischko*, a huge brick oven. Two-inch thick boards covered the top of the *prischko* and three generations of the same family might sleep on top of it. In the wintertime it was terrific because the stove was fired up during the day for cooking and heating, and during the night the bricks radiated back the warmth.

In the summertime we seldom saw leather shoes, most peasants wore homemade, woven footwear. In the winter months all of the Russians wore thick cotton pants, a heavy jacket, a pelt, fur cap and heavy felt boots called *valenki*; you couldn't tell female from male.

Our move north took us past Vyaz'ma to the little town of Chatsk (Gzhatsk), near Rzhev, where we were placed in reserve. We came to that area in October and in the beginning we slept in tents made from the triangular-shaped rain shelters each of us carried. Four shelters lashed together made a tent large enough for four men.

We built ourselves bunkers because all of the houses in the village had been burnt to the ground except one that became the company kitchen. Each gun had a shovel mounted on a hinged steel panel located below the barrel. When necessary we dropped this panel down so that we couldn't be shot at from underneath the gun. We took our gun shovel, that of our half-track, and our trenching tools and began cutting into the dark soil. We were trying to finish our bunkers before the winter of '42 set in for good, but we didn't make it. The bunkers measured 3 x 4 yards and were set about 3 yards into the ground and they were not finished until after the first snow fell. Sometimes in the morning only the tip of our temporary shelters were visible and we had to shovel our way out of the tent past the snow.

We seldom used mines in our perimeter defense, although we always carried between four and eight T-mines with us. We only used mines when we were by ourselves in what we referred to as the *Igel* "hedgehog" defense. In those instances, after our bunker was finished we would dig out enough ground so that the gun barrel was level with the surrounding terrain. We encircled the gun with a trench, several small ammo bunkers, and a latrine. This enabled us to defend ourselves from every direction. We put *Tellerminen* in that area where we expected a frontal assault from Russian tanks.

We were never instructed on mines at Herford but we quickly learned on the battlefield how to insert the primers and locate an armed mine. You could walk on a T-mine and it wouldn't do anything to you but if a truck or a tank rolled over it the pressure on the top fuse ignited twelve pounds of explosive. There were two primers, and the one underneath attached to a steel wire served as an anchor and as a trigger so that no one could lift up the mine without detonating it. To remove a mine you had to dig all the way around it until you could get your fingers underneath to loosen or disconnect the steel wire prior to lifting the mine, or it exploded in your face.

Away from our bunker we dug shallow U-shaped depressions for our vehicles. We would drive our half-tracks in, cover the top with straw and place a straw mat over the back. At night we took turns starting the engine every hour and running it for about fifteen minutes.

Whenever a Russian artillery barrage hit, dirt filtered through the overhead mass of logs and soil. Even in winter the dust was in everyone's hair, eyes and lungs. If you were eating, a mouthful of grit seasoned each bite. To overcome this inconvenience we hung our rain shelters on the underside of the ceiling.

The garments of anyone returning from outside were caked with balls of snow that slowly released the scent of wet wool into the dry warm air. The darkened interior of the bunkers was sharply scented by the stench of unwashed bodies, cigarettes and wood smoke, and the lighter smell of gun oil. The small containers of Russian gun oil were highly prized, jealously guarded, and never wasted. In extreme low temperatures our gun oil would become sluggish. But even the coldest weather never seemed to affect the Russian oil.

Candles and a small lamp called a Hindenburg light lit our bunkers. The Hindenburg lights were simple, round cartons containing wax and a wick. They were about 2.5 inches across and about .5 inches high. Even with the candles there was too little light to take photos inside without a flash. To overcome this I cut open a flare and scraped some of the magnesium powder into a scrap of newspaper. I twisted the newspaper together very tightly and dipped it into gasoline. It burned hot and fast and scorched your fingers, but it worked.

We had little stoves fired by hardened methylated spirit that were just big enough to support your mess gear. My mother sent me packets of instant pudding and all I had to do was stir in water and heat the mixture on my stove. Outside in the summertime the stove wasn't any problem, however in the wintertime, inside the bunker, the fuel gave everyone an unpleasant taste in their mouth.

Harsh winter winds soon rearranged the snowfall into hard crusty drifts. A thick mound of snow, broken only by the stovepipe, concealed our bunker and all the telltale signs of its construction. When it was cloudless a harsh winter brightness filled the short daylight hours. During such days the sun illuminated yet never warmed even the most brightly lit corners. On one cold, sunny day I took my *Vogtlander* camera outside and recorded this scene.

While posted near Rzhev we constructed a secondary line of defense in case the Russians broke through. In our area there were lots of tall young trees about 12 to 21 feet high. We cut them down and faced the crowns of the trees in the direction from which the Russians would attack us. When you put trees over trees, side by side, and several on top of one another it produces quite a wall. This was something new to us. We were accustomed to barbed wire. However, we knew that it was nearly impossible for enemy infantry to overcome our close-set tree tops. We had tried it.

Because it was early December we built a fire where we would come from time to time to warm our feet and hands while smoking a cigarette. On one occasion there were six or seven of us standing around the fire with men from other units, including a sergeant and a corporal. At some distance we saw a group of officers approaching and before I knew it most of the men around the fire had disappeared. The officers neared to about ten yards but nobody made any attempt to acknowledge their presence so I took it upon myself to report to them. I walked over to their group, brought myself to attention and gave my name, rank, company and finished by stating that we were a work group.

I recognized that the officer I was addressing, who was somewhat smaller than the others and wearing a monocle, was

Colonel General Model. Model took my report and asked questions on several details concerning the defenses we were constructing. I explained as much as I could and then he told me to go back to the fire and warm myself. I saluted, and returned to the fire. When I looked back they had walked off.

Everyone who had been around the fire reappeared, including the sergeant. They clapped me on my shoulder and congratulated me. I felt that I had simply done what all of us had been instructed to do as new recruits at Herford—always report to visiting officers and give an account of your duties.

I received my first award in Rzhev on December 11, 1942. It was for the summer campaign of that year and required that you had participated in at least six battles. We had arrived in Gustaya two weeks too late to receive the Eastern Front Medal. This medal was for everyone who had participated in the first winter campaign of 1941. It was popularly known as the *Gefrierfleish* or frozen meat medal.

It was around this time that we were issued our first cold weather gear with one side white and the other printed with a mottled spring camouflage pattern. It didn't come too soon. The winter snows had long since transformed the landscape.

Russia, summer 1942. A Russian church with the 95th Division cemetery near Kolpny.

Gzhatsk, Russia, September 1942.

Rzhev, Russia, 1942–1943. The stovepipe of the Rzhev bunker.

Rzhev, Russia, 1942–1943. Entrance to the Rzhev bunker.

Rzhev, Russia, 1942–1943. Interior of the bunker at Rzhev.

Rzhev, Russia, 1942–1943. Averbeck, right.

Rzhev, Russia, 1942–1943. Returning from an engagement with Russian T-34s.

Rzhev, Russia, 1942–1943.

CHAPTER III

1943
An Iron Portion

My first furlough from Russia came in January 1943 while we were in the area of Sychevka, just south of Rzhev. We had to walk 10 miles to the railroad station. It was a clear night with a full moon and minus 48 degrees. Each of us carried two heavy bags along with our rifles and gas masks. We were not allowed to take our new winter jacket and insulated pants. Anyone going on furlough turned in this gear to their supply officer. When I returned, mine had been "stolen."

We traveled by train to a *Delausung* station and rid ourselves of our winter guests. After my delousing and a health check, I was given a 20-pound parcel of sugar, flour, oil, fat, and sausage.

Twenty-one-day furloughs officially started after reaching Germany because sometimes it required three to four days of travel to reach our border. My train ride to Münster took 20 hours. Back home everything was strictly rationed and my food package made a welcome gift.

My mother didn't trust the *Delausung* and she made me get into the washroom tub where I rescrubbed myself. In her determination to make doubly sure my clothing was not secreting an unwanted louse she heated a large kettle of water and boiled all my underclothes and uniform.

The British bombed Münster almost every night and I hated the air raid sirens warning of their arrival. The alarms sounded and everyone hurried to their preassigned shelters. My mother, sister, and myself went along with my girlfriend and her two younger brothers to an old cellar used for growing mushrooms. There were three rooms in that cellar and we always thought that we were pretty safe. But after a year away from home, I discovered that I felt safer on the *HKL*. On the front line you usually heard the incoming artillery or machine gun fire. Certainly, no one ever has the opportunity to listen to the one that wounds or kills. But I was more at ease at the front than in my bed at home. I could sleep on the front line and nothing disturbed me. Nothing that is, as long as it was a sound generated by one of us. Whenever someone approached who was not of our group, whether friend or enemy, I was instantly awake and alert.

The day after my return I encountered the electrician under whom I had been apprenticing. While talking he asked me what my plans were for after the war. I said that I was going to remain in the army for twelve years and afterwards sign up for another twelve. In this way I could apply for a good civil service job upon leaving the service.

He reflected and said, "Let's be honest, it doesn't look to me like we are winning the war."

All I could do was look at him.

"From my point of view," he continued, "we have lost the war already. My advice to you would be to return to trade school and finish your electrician's apprenticeship."

I responded that I felt pretty uneasy about returning because I had left so abruptly in 1941.

"Nonetheless," he encouraged me, "try it anyway."

What I hadn't said, was that I was not too keen about attending class because this meant even less time with my girlfriend and family. Overnight I gave it some thought and the next morning I went to the electricians' school. I was surprised to discover that my instructor was still there. He was a major in the air force, and he had secured leave from active duty to continue instructing apprentices. When he saw me he was all smiles, gave me a warm welcome, and asked what had happened since I had left school, the places I had been and so on. After answering his questions I mentioned that my former employer had suggested that I complete my requirements for the journeyman's license. I was further surprised when he said that he was all for it and that I was to come back to school the next day.

When I had joined the military, I was nearly finished with my electrician's apprenticeship. To complete my training, I followed an intensive three-week program, with two days of school per week. The rest of the time I worked for my old employer. One afternoon, during a break in class work, I was outside having a cigarette when from behind an instructor delivered a stinging slap to the side of my head. I was taken inside and given a dressing down that didn't seem to have an end until, at one moment, I was allowed to show my military identification. The correction turned into apologies and I was requested to please smoke in an area hidden from the other students. Smoking was a new habit I had acquired on the front line, and it had nothing to do with poor morals or an absence of correct behavior. After a year in Russia, I had a difficult time adjusting to their code of ideal student conduct. I had involuntarily absorbed the realities of my battlefield experiences. I had made those experiences a part of myself, as had many other teenagers, and I would never be a schoolboy again.

At the end of the third week three master electricians judged my oral, written, and practical work, and agreed that I should be licensed as a journeyman electrician.

My furlough had passed far too quickly. Münster's railway station was teaming with soldiers and their families and I was quietly pleased when my father and I discovered that our train was more than full. I quickly suggested we go to the station master and get stamps permitting us to catch a transport the following day. But my father, who was also returning to his unit, refused and said that we could sit in a passageway on our gear. I was angry, I would have enjoyed another 24 hours with my girlfriend.

When I returned to the front everything was as I had left it. Inside the bunker the pale, flickering glow of Hindenburg lights irregularly lit all the smiling familiar faces. Everything else was lost in the confining darkness of our dugout. On January 31 General Paulus surrendered at Stalingrad and the comments of my former employer came immediately to mind. Shortly afterwards we began a long series of withdrawals.

On our way southeast from Sechefka we never knew exactly when we would have to gather our gear and pull out. Sometimes we were retreating daily, at other times every couple of days. A week would be the most time we would stay in one position before moving again.

Our withdrawals were always very orderly. One division in the back would build up a defensive line and then our division, for example, would break off from the Russians. We never had anything to really fear or any reason to look over our shoulders. We always knew that the Russians were behind us, but not in fighting strength, at first.

During our withdrawal we stopped briefly at Doroghubuz on the Dnieper River where we located our gun on the hill above the railway station. Elements of the 95th's infantry were about 1,000 yards in front of us. The enemy was expected at any time so when we were building our bunker and trenches each was designed along the hedgehog fortress concept. We forced our way into the deep set frost using a couple of sledge hammers and a big iron rod.

During the day the sun was warm enough to soften a few inches of topsoil, below that we had to go to work with our tools. The first couple of weeks the Russians were not there yet, so we were working nearly 24 hours a day. We built our bunker first so that we had something over our heads and were out of the elements. Salvaged materials from some nearby abandoned houses made a strong, layered wooden ceiling. We liked to have several layers of wood, each one six to seven inches thick over us, with soil in between. By the time we started digging trenches and a little bunker for ammunition, we worked only during the night because the Russians had caught up to us and were occupying a bluff overlooking our new front line. They could not reach us with machine gun fire—but we had a lot of respect for their artillery.

While under fire the earth around you literally shakes. It didn't matter how hard the soil was frozen, great hollows would be scooped out of it and vaporous tendrils would waft slowly out of the hole each one rooted to hot metal fragments and bits of sudden-heated earth. Steam also rises from freshly torn flesh of what was once a horse or a friend. Tremors from the blasts constantly shifted the soil above the bunker and dust would filter through the layers of logs and collect on our tarpaulins suspended from the ceiling. Anything hanging overhead was set into a pendulum-like motion.

When we had finished our fortifications everybody thought that now, at last, we would be able to take it easy but new marching orders came almost immediately. Our company abandoned its new positions and, later, quite a few others like it.

While building our fortifications there were indications that spring was not far off. The disappearing snow chafed by a warm wind, revealed the castoff wastes of our residence. Discarded shell casings were mixed with bits and pieces of unidentifiable metal parts and human waste. Spring has an odor all its own formed from warming soils, the previous autumn's decaying leaves, and budding plants. When the wind was right the pungent odor of death made its unwelcome contribution.

The long shadows stretching over the winter snows gave way, seemingly overnight, to mosaic-like pieces of blue sky reflected in water-filled depressions. The white tarp draping the gun barrel was removed and stored away. To take its place, we cut willow and birch branches budded out in yellow-green that were perfect for camouflage although they required regular renewal.

Mud adhered to everything. Thick coatings of mud obscured undercarriages, sucked noisily at wheels and made a man's foot bulbous with its weighty mass.

Once in a while, when the *HKL* was quiet, it was possible to go back to divisional headquarters, some ten miles behind the front, to see a film or civilian entertainers. This occurred very seldom. We generally entertained ourselves. One fellow played the accordion and Eric Puppa played his guitar and sang.

On the *HKL* we celebrated Christmas, New Year, and Easter and on these occasions we usually received something special with our rations. If the whole company was together and out on the front line our cooks would try to organize an exceptional dinner or bake cakes but this too did not happen very often.

On Tuesday, April 20, 1943, we received a special ration of rum and coffee in celebration of Hitler's birthday. We were excited because we were given about two ounces of real coffee beans. We put the beans in a cloth sack and beat it with a hammer. Then we had the wondrous idea to mix a generous amount of sugar with the coffee and rum. In our drunkenness we left our positions and walked tipsily along the top of our trenches in full view of the Russians. It was a very stupid thing to do and luckily nobody shot at us. Afterwards, whenever I was issued coffee I would make a small packet and send it home. My mother used the coffee like currency.

It was at Doroghubuz that we adopted an existing outhouse for use as our latrine. We sat there, pants around our ankles, facing the Russian line. We were safe because we knew we were just out of rifle range. One afternoon when everyone was inside the bunker a friend left for the toilet. While he was gone there was a shrill rumble and the explosion of a shell hitting right beside us. We rushed outside and discovered the latrine had disappeared. The Russian projectile had hit the berm behind the outhouse blasting our friend from his perch where he had been reading a long letter from his girlfriend. He was unhurt with the exception of a small bit of shrapnel lodged in his scrotum. There was not even enough of a wound to send him home. After that, whenever he set off to the latrine we never missed the opportunity to laugh at his expense.

In the summertime the sun was hot and the roads were dry and dusty, and for the time being we escaped the lice. That summer they sent us south-southeast towards Orel in the Ukraine to join Army Group Center and the 9th Army under the command of Field Marshal Model.

Along our way southeast we passed through the city of Rostovel where, for the first time, we encountered roads of macadam. All the rest were impassable mud holes when raining, or frozen and full of teeth jarring potholes. The arterials in the Moscow area were the only exception and these were cobblestone.

Russian winter offensives in the Ukraine had created a salient 110 miles long and 60 miles deep into our line at Kursk on the Seim River between Orel and Belgorod. In mid-June the *95 Infanterie Division* and its "thirteenth company" the 195th were to support a summer offensive bent on eliminating the Kursk bulge.

The weather was pleasantly warm. Although we were somewhat familiar with the area from the previous summer the Orel-Kursk countryside presented us with a striking contrast to the confines of the northern forests we had recently departed. An immense sky dominated the open plains of the rolling landscape. A low horizon stretched from left to right as far as you could see.

We were 80 miles north of the main battle area and barely 60 miles northwest of Gustaya, our position during the winter of 1941–1942. Repeatedly postponed, the attack ultimately began in earnest early Monday morning, July 5, 1943.

We joined two other guns in camouflaged positions in a wheat field covering a shallow gulch, right on the edge of the front line. Behind us were two *Panzer Sturmgeschutzs*, each equipped with the short-barreled 75 mm cannon. Without a turret, their main gun was capable of only five to six degrees movement left and right of center. Targets to either side of that field required the assault gun to change position. We got behind our cannons and waited. Then the unbelievable happened.

On the opposite ridge of the little gulch where we were located, four T-34s drove up and stopped less than 500 yards from us. They were just sitting there, engines idling, when the *Sturmgeschutzs*, out of sight on the reverse slope of the hill behind us, opened up. Their 75 mm shells whooshed over our heads exploding harmlessly around the Russian tanks. Immediately, the four started returning fire onto what they presumed to be the positions of our assault guns.

Behind, and in front of us, the grain field was erupting in brilliant flashes of hot orange. We sat there avoiding any movement that would give us away. When you are a gun leader in the field it is in your discretion when to open or hold fire. On this occasion our gun leader had orders requiring permission from the company officer to shoot. With four prime targets well within the effective range of our 75 mm AT rounds, the corporal must have sensed our anxiousness, but he was unwilling to take an independent decision and countermand his fire orders. Instead, he ordered me to formally request permission to engage the enemy tanks.

I crawled away through the rows of grain, trying my best not to reveal our gun to the Russian tankers. Our company commander was about 1,000 yards behind us. I had to go up the hill and over the top before I was out of sight on the reverse slope. In the meantime the Russians began shooting with big 222 mm guns. Their artillery was effectively covering the whole ridge. When I went up that hump I was on my belly for over 200 yards.

I prayed as I crawled up the hillside that I was invisible to the Soviet gunners and to their exploding shells. The violence of each explosion was terrific. Dark clumps of earth flew skyward and dropped heavily back into the field only to be freshly wrenched from their rest and tossed about again. When I gained the hilltop I stood up and broke into a run past the *Sturmgeschutzs* until reaching the command post.

I explained what the situation was to our commander and he said go back and tell the corporal to start shooting. As I neared the hilltop on my return, everything was strangely quiet. In the interval marked by my absence, the Russian tanks had departed—none were destroyed. I was angered I had been made to risk my life for a missed opportunity born of indecision. Quite often this kind of order seemed to coincide with good situations and indecisive gun leaders who wouldn't take matters into their own hands or have the courage to shoot.

In my defense I would further say that talk had been circulating. One of these rumors recounted how an order was given not to shoot and when the situation developed differently than headquarter's was seeing it, several enemy tanks were destroyed due to the initiative of the antitank crew leader. I reasoned that through insubordination you risked losing rank or getting the Iron Cross. I, and others, felt that the latter outweighed the perils of countermanding orders.

Our offensive failed. By July 12, after seven days of battle, the Russians had successfully blunted our attempts to pinch close the opening to their bulge, and they counterattacked.

When the Americans and their allies landed in Italy, forces already committed to the Kursk battle were diverted south and the July offensive, in our area, became defensive. By August 5 the cities of Orel and Belgorod were in Russian hands.

It didn't take long when facing a Russian tank attack that was not supported by infantry, to realize the importance of eliminating the larger and more powerful KVIs and IIs bringing up the rear. However, we couldn't afford to expose ourselves to the T-34s that were in the middle between us and their rear guard. There was no sure or safe way of combatting the frontal armor of a tank. An antitank crew that was discovered by a Soviet tanker was in serious trouble. Consequently, we developed a tactic that allowed us to use our camouflage and weapon to our advantage.

In their assembly areas the Russian tanks were a group. But when they closed their hatches and crossed their line of departure, each tank became an individual. Without radios each one depended on the eyes and ears of its crew and these were all directed towards the front. Even with this in mind, you never got used to sitting there watching the dark squat forms of the T-34s rolling towards you, followed by the bulkier shapes of the KVs, without a sharp anxiety unrelieved by the absolute trustworthiness of the men crouching beside you.

The T-34s advanced and soon you could hear the squeal of metal tracks and the growl of engines. Our anxious eyes followed each tank watching to make certain that no one's head suddenly appeared from a hatch. The irregular squeal of the tracks mixed with the threat of discovery raised the hair on our necks. For the moment, we were the quarry, they were the hunters, and time or at least our sense of time slowly dilated. Seconds became minutes and minutes could feel like eternity.

The menacing shapes got bigger and bigger and all the while we were hoping that they would not change their courses forcing us to break the secrecy of our camouflage. But none did. The tanks pressed the high grasses aside and, underneath, the tracks worked like mechanical molds imprinting their regular patterns into the soil. Each moved noisily past us. Each vibrated the ground with its passage. The growl of their engines was now behind us but the tenseness of our situation hung in an air thick with the scent of tank exhaust.

The KVIs and IIs bringing up the rear were waiting for one of us to reveal ourselves to their gunners. From our low vantage point their silhouettes looked huge. The earth trembled again as they groaned up to our position and noisily bypassed us. No one moved for fear of being detected. The constant fear of discovery further tightened already aching stomachs. Eyes continually searched for infantry or a change in the pattern of the advance.

When the last one passed us, it was as though our breathing had resumed and a new sense of time, a quickened time, collapsed upon us. We jumped up, brought the spars of the carriage together, and heaved the gun around so that we were facing the departing tanks. Now we were the hunter with certain targets.

We spread the spars and the gunner looked through the sight while a shell was lifted into the breech. A second of quiet was followed by the firing of the gun. The 75 mm shell tore into the nearest rear engine compartment, blasting its way through the power plant. The explosion stopped the KVI in its tracks. It was the last tank in the advance and the others that were beginning to burst into flames were unaware of the activity behind them. After cutting through the KVs we turned our guns on the T-34s.

When firing from behind a shot that was too long was perceived by the Soviet tanker as one fired from in front that was too short. This brought about a great deal of confusion when the lead tankers would suddenly discover the tanks to their left and right going up in smoke. And while they searched for the source of the explosion before them, behind their tank an armor piercing shell was already streaking forward ready to explode into their interior.

The 75 had an even longer and larger muzzle brake than our old 50s. The cross vents of the brake evenly directed the muzzle gases to either side of the barrel end thereby reducing or "braking" the recoil. Nonetheless, the blast from the main barrel caused the gun carriage to hop on its wheels pushing the ends of the spars spread behind it into the ground. Another shell was slid into the breech and locked in place. We quickly turned our heads, and hands instinctively reached to cover ears as each round was fired. Before a casing had stopped smoking another shell was in the breech and two more were being handed up.

Each explosion stilled an engine and each sent black oily smoke erupting from every opening of the T-34s until they were engulfed in a dark hot cloud. Our continuous firing kept the air vibrating, ultimately desensitizing the ears to anything but the loudest of noises.

Two small cranks turned in or out corrected the aim. Our gunner whirled one crank, adjusted another, re-sighted the cannon on a tank engine and within seconds it too was on fire; a second round accelerated its destruction.

When you are standing right beside it, the blast of a cannon is deafening. The spent casing comes flying out of the breech and another takes its place. A quick look by our gunner in the range finder reconfirmed the target, and his palm pressed the firing mechanism. A second later another brass casing flew to the ground and the whole action was repeated. The blast of the gun was a reassuring sound—confirmation that we were still operating, still alive, and still fighting. Our furiously rapid action resuscitated us after nearly suffocating from tense immobility.

We always said that you never heard the one that would kill you. This was a small consolation. A direct hit by a T-34 would demolish a 75 and its crew. Guns halved by the explosion added razor-sharp metal bits to the destructive power of high explosive tank shells. Afterwards I would find a foot in a boot here or bits of cloth or flesh there. Our number and unit were stamped two times on the face of a thin metal oval worn around the neck. When someone was killed we snapped it in two. One half went to headquarters, the other remained with its owner to await collection and burial.

Hermann Jahr, a friend of mine who was a farmer and really needed his arms and legs in those days of horse and plow, always feared he would lose them. I saw his gun hit by direct tank fire. When I got there only a glistening gelatinous-looking ribbon of red flesh supported his right forearm. I reached for the scissors I always carried in my tunic pocket and then hesitated. I applied a tourniquet around the upper arm and I laid the lower part over his rib cage before bandaging everything in place. Suddenly he screamed, "My arm! My arm!" I took his left hand and placed it on the piece strapped to his chest and said, "Here it is." Hermann was evacuated and I never heard if he survived.

After the battle we returned the guns to their original firing positions, restored the camouflage around the front, cleaned up the shells littering our site and waited for the next attack. Behind us black columns of smoke rose skyward above the hulks of burning tanks. Exploding ammunition punctuated the roar of the fires and tossed unexploded rounds into the surrounding field. Blackened wrecks would still be warm the following day.

When given enough time, we dug foxholes to provide another level of safety. When Russian tankers overran a position they would park on foxholes. The driver would set first one track and then the other in gear causing the tank to twist in place. The alternating track motion ground away at the soil and whomever was secreted there. We always dug our individual foxholes in a L-shape. They couldn't cover the whole thing with their tracks and we could get out beside the tank where we were invisible.

Everyone carried rations popularly called our *Eisen Portione*, or "iron portion." It consisted of one can of lard with pork meat and one can of hard biscuits, and it was strictly forbidden to eat this ration except in emergencies. Anyone caught eating their iron portion when there wasn't an emergency could be court-martialed. Mind you, "If you got caught."

Either during long battles or immediately after an engagement when we had a quiet moment again, we ate our "iron portion" of food. Naturally you had to report their consumption or loss. This was always done with a short letter to the company or the division stating why you didn't have these rations any longer. Our standard letter was, "Destroyed through enemy artillery fire." I'm sure 99 percent of the time they didn't believe us. However, no action was ever taken and we were always resupplied.

In the fall of 1943, after everything had quieted down on the front line, we were sent to Bryansk and then southwest towards

Gomel by railroad. We got off the railroad cars there and sat for about a week before receiving new orders that sent us northwest to Byshow.

How to get out of Russia was on everyone's mind. Each time they put us on flatbed rail cars everybody was saying, "Good, at last they are shipping us down to France." A train moving in a westerly direction during the day inspired plenty of hope—based on rumor. And it never failed that during the night it always changed direction and the next morning we were again going either north or east.

Our retreats maintained their orderliness. One division was holding about 20 miles in the back while we would disengage from the Russians, filter through our line, and then we would wait for the division in front to come back. At this time contact with the Russian's advance elements was limited.

We got pretty adept at predicting moves. The week before a pullout we received chocolate, vodka, and cigarettes. Those were things we didn't often see in our daily or weekly rations. When we got our chocolate and the rest we knew that we should get ourselves ready and all of our gear in order because soon we would be on the move again. And it never failed.

By Wednesday, August 18, we completed our withdrawal to the *Bolvastellung* in the vicinity of Zhizda. The *Bolvastellung* was a hastily erected line of defense on the western side of the Desna and Bolva rivers.

The Russian autumn had quickly shaken loose the dark shades of summer. The crowns of trees turned yellow in the crisp air and the molding forest floor hardened itself anticipating the snows to come. On September 25, Smolensk fell to Soviet forces.

We very seldom received newspapers in Russia. The only exception were those sent by our families. The tank corps had a newspaper called the *Panzerfaust* or Tank Fist with a drawing of an armored fist on the top of the front page. Antitank crews didn't have a regular newspaper and I saw one of the tankers maybe two times. News from home was gleaned from letters.

The halt of our nearly two-month long withdrawal allowed our mail to catch up with us. I received one particularly memorable letter from my mother. It concerned the American bombing raid of Sunday, October 10, 1943. By 1943 the Americans bombed more and more frequently during the day, while the British kept up their runs during the night. On Sunday, October 10, while my sister was at work, there was a heavy daytime bombing raid and so my mother went to her bomb shelter. There was only one entrance to the old mushroom growing cellars that served as our refuge. Upon entering, you came into an anteroom where there were three different doors leading into shelters One, Two, and Three. We were always in number Three on the far right-hand side. My mother was headed into it when a neighbor woman called to her asking, "Mrs. Averbeck, why don't you come with us?" That saved her life. Our cellar received direct hits and rooms Two and Three collapsed completely, killing most of the people sheltering there.

Shelter One also collapsed, but the exploding pressure wave didn't hit that room as fiercely as the others. The destruction left my mother up to her shoulders in debris, only her head was exposed and above that was daylight. Rescue crews checking for survivors pulled her from the rubble.

When the air raid alarm sounded my sister went to a hospital shelter near where she worked. Several direct hits struck the hospital but my sister came out of it alive.

My girlfriend was in a movie theater that took a direct hit, collapsing one wall. From the seats you could see right into the adjoining street. She made it out unscathed, however she somehow lost her shoes.

Once a month, soldiers received a two pound parcel stamp for use by their families. Sometimes parcels from home were slow in finding their way to the front. One such package came late and the butter in it was rancid so I used it to fry potatoes. Before the larger parcel stamp was made available to families, the weight limit was set at 100 grams, about three ounces. Families could send as many 100 gram packets as they wanted with no restrictions. But what can you put in such tiny parcels? My mother solved the problem with what I consider to be an ingenious solution. She would bake a cake and then carefully divide it into 100 gram portions. Or she would barter on the blackmarket for air-dried or smoked sausage. Sometimes she would have ten to fifteen little packages all connected together by a single cord. I received several of these. On days when we had mail call, the person distributing the mail would reach into the sack and lifting an envelope or packet, call out its owner's name. All of my mother's little packets strung together came to be known as Averbeck's convoy. Everyone always shared everything possible and my friends on our gun were always happy when another of my convoys arrived.

My aunt worked in the parcel office. She told my mother that when preparing packages she should rub wax over the stamp after attaching it to the wrapping, and that I should return all stamps. I returned the stamp in my next letter although I had no idea why I should. When my mother got it she covered the stamp with newspaper and ironed it. The wax melted and with it the post office cancellation mark. The now uncancelled stamp was steamed off the paper and before I knew it I had another parcel, much to my surprise and the envy of my friends.

We were always on the lookout for some way to supplement our daily rations. Usually the homes in villages closer to the front were deserted. Either the population had left with the Russians in 1941 or they were departing after we arrived. In such cases, we often found little kitchen gardens with fresh tomatoes, potatoes, and onions. Sometimes there were also a few apples.

The *Spiess Oberfeldwebel* kept us in food and the best of everything he possibly could within any given situation. This was well demonstrated at the end of October 1943 when we were once more put on flatbed railcars with our guns and half-tracks and began shuffling around from one rail yard to the next. We spent about a week on the flatbeds. To make life easier we nailed our tents to the floorboards because we were sleeping right on the train.

Early one morning we arrived in a large rail yard where we were to wait until the following day. In the late afternoon a freight train slowly approached and stopped beside us. There were a lot of soldiers on board and when the train stopped they all took up guard posts left and right, front and back of their train. Naturally we were immediately suspicious and asked them, "What outfit are you?" And, "Where are you coming from?"

They replied that they were in charge of supplies for officers' clubs, and that they were being transferred to a new area but that they didn't know where to yet. When word circulated that they had food on the train our goal was to get to it.

Our first step was to inform the *Spiess Oberfeldwebel* that the train was stocked with food. After some reflection he went over to the sergeant in charge of the boxcars and got acquainted. Through a series of questions he learned that this unit was almost always on the move and recently had not had an opportunity to rest.

Our *Spiess* asked, "Why should we post double guards? You could take the outside line of your train and we could take the outside line of ours and everyone could get some rest."

Their sergeant felt that this proposal was a blessing.

"By the way," our *Spiess* warned him, "we are expecting to receive our gas shipment tonight. It will have to be distributed to all the half-tracks on the flatbeds, so there will be some commotion later."

"No problem," he replied. "I'll let my men know so that they don't interfere."

Around ten o'clock we crossed over to the first boxcar and quietly broke it open. In the dark all we could see was that it was loaded. But with what? One of our dispatchers climbed inside and was standing on a wooden barrel when suddenly the top gave way and he was immersed in honey. Two men had to climb aboard and pull him out of the morass. He never recovered his boots. In the meantime we opened several more cars and in one we found crates and crates of fresh eggs. Each crate held 144 eggs. Everybody was carrying two to three crates to their rail car and hiding them in their tents. To cover our trail as we were going back and forth, we carried on "conversations" based on questions and answers such as, "Hey I've got two cans of gasoline which gun needs this?" Which would inspire an appropriate and equally false statement.

In one boxcar we found neatly tinned butterfat, crates of meat, and chocolate. Soon we had plenty of provisions on the flatbed where I slept.

Our company leader had been kept in the dark about what was going on. Drawn by the activity he asked the *Spiess* why the men were running about? When he was told that we were receiving gasoline, he shrugged it off, mumbling as he departed that he had not seen that order. After an hour and a half everything quieted down and we were anxiously waiting and wondering who was leaving first.

Around four o'clock the next morning, while it was still dark, the signal came to get ready to move out. In accordance with the agreement of the previous night, our *Spiess* notified the others that in 15 minutes we were leaving and that they should repost all their guards. Just after daybreak we departed.

With full light our train was steadily under way and the egg shells were flying from the left and right. Every gun crew was equipped with a stove that we referred to as a cannon oven. It was small, about 10 inches in diameter, and you could burn just about anything in it. At that moment we were burning coal because there was plenty to be collected from the rail yards we were passing through. Everyone's oven was smoking and everyone was cooking eggs. The eggs were a real treat. It was one of the few occasions I ate fresh eggs during the whole time I was in Russia.

If you could shield yourself from the gritty black smoke of the engine, the clean morning air was refreshing and our company leader was outside when the egg shells caught his attention. He asked his valet, "Halt Auf Der Heide, did we receive eggs in our rations? If so, I would like to have some now."

"No sir, we didn't receive any eggs."

"Then how come the others are throwing egg shells from the beds by the dozens?"

"Well," he replied, "yesterday the men went with salt into the Russian village and exchanged it for fresh eggs."

"In that case at the next stop go to the kitchen, request a pound of salt and get me some fresh eggs too."

It was over a month before he knew what we had done. I will never forget the look on his face when we finally told him. He was an elderly man who was on the board of directors for a coal mine. He had been called up from the reserves and was not a professional soldier.

Once off the train, we again found ourselves building and rebuilding bunkers. We were far enough from the front for our activities to assume some routine and too close to let our guard down. This time, however, we stole a case of dynamite and used half sticks of the explosive to excavate the frozen ground for our *Igel* defense works.

Eric Puppa was gathering lumber from a ruin to be picked up by the half-track for transport to our building site. After assembling a few loads he took the opportunity to nap. When the driver returned he backed into the open side of the structure pinning a screaming Eric under one of the tracks. Eric was hopeful that both thigh bones were broken. As it turned out, nothing was broken or even fractured although the cuts and bruises were painful. To his dismay the accident was not severe enough to be sent home. He was transported back to a Warsaw hospital with another man from our company. Eric quickly became the favorite of the nurses. Even after he had recovered they didn't want to let him, his voice, or guitar depart.

While at the hospital, they spent their day passes visiting town. The difficulty was that they were penniless. This was remedied by stealing a hospital blanket. One would stake out a city corner and surreptitiously propose the blanket for sale to passing Poles. When the sale was complete, the other would locate himself in the path of the departing Pole. When the victim neared a badge was flashed, and pretending to be a policeman in search of contraband, the blanket was confiscated. The unsuspecting civilian was allowed to go free after a stern warning that black marketeering was a dangerous and forbidden business. The blanket was sold until the two had enough money to fund their day out.

Every day we rotated our guard duty. For example I, with someone else, would stand guard 10:00 P.M. to 12:00 midnight, the next day 12:00 to 2:00 A.M., and then 2:00 to 4:00, and 4:00 to 6:00. Day after day it changed automatically without anyone fussing or asking questions. Some nights double guard duty was necessary and we stood the first two and the last two shifts. The only difference was that in the wintertime with 20 to 40 degree below zero temperatures, you were able to be out half-an-hour at the most, but still we went out two guys together. In between shifts you either were in a Russian house or in your bunker. With only two hours off you couldn't really sleep well. You dozed until it was your turn to go outside again.

We wore paths through each new snow cover. Some led to our gun emplacements, others to the area used as a latrine, still others to our command post in the rear. The hard packed, uneven surfaces guided us over the least circuitous routes saving time and energy when a situation demanded it most.

In Russia we wore our uniforms from one vacation to the next and you never knew when you might receive another furlough. You slept in your uniform and the only thing you changed was your underwear. You washed your underwear yourself and sometimes for several weeks you didn't have any possibility to do so, especially in the wintertime when there was no way to dry your clothes. Consequently, whenever we were in a village I was always keen to use the *banya* or sauna.

Most villages had *banyas*. Generally this was a little wooden community building located beside a creek. We went in together with the Russians for whom the *banya* was a family bath. Inside, the men, women, and children could be found sitting together. Water poured on the stones sent steam clouds rolling outwards over our naked figures. The damp warmth of the steam filled your lungs and opened the pores of your skin so that you wiped away a week's dirt along with the lice that had made you their home. Sometimes the younger girls would wield leafy birch branches that were stockpiled for use during the wintertime. When the intensely moist heat had loosened up your pores the youngest girls circulated swatting you with the branches. We often hit one another with the branches as well, but whenever the girls were in there they performed this task. There was no sexual harassment in that steam chamber. In fact, that was the furthest thing from your mind. Once again in the dressing room, a clean change of underwear was firmly held in place by a soiled uniform. And the lice that had patiently waited in the clothing hung in the warm antechamber wriggled back, renewing their acquaintance with their hosts.

We had just arrived in a village when some of my friends called, "Hey Bernhard, the *banya* is smoking," meaning that it was usable. I had nothing to do so I took my clean underwear and walked to the *banya*. When I opened the door I entered a small antechamber maybe two yards long and the width of the log cabin. On this occasion I saw overcoats, pants, and footwear on the floor. It was impossible to tell from the clothes hanging there if the owners were female, or male, or both. Besides we had done it dozens of times before and never had problems. On seeing the clothing I thought only that villagers were inside.

I got undressed. When I opened the door to enter the steam room I discovered that someone had just poured water on the stones. The whole room was steamed up and I couldn't see a thing. I closed the door behind me, and took one step forward waiting for the steam to clear. I didn't want to be rude and step on someone. The moment the steam cleared I heard the excited yells of eight or nine women who upon seeing me covered themselves with their hands. The screams paralyzed me and instead of turning and leaving I stood there like a dumb fool not knowing what to do. It took me several seconds to take stock of what had happened before I left and got dressed again. When I emerged from the antechamber I was greeted by my gun crew rolling with laughter. They had seen the women go in and had sent me in for a laugh. They had a good laugh, and I had a red face. After the women went home I returned and took my sauna.

Christmas passed uneventfully and afterwards we were ordered to travel about 30 miles to a new position. While preparing to leave the village an army truck arrived. The driver and his comrade in the cab asked if we might be going in the same direction they were and whether or not we could accompany them because the area was full of partisans. We agreed and they led the way.

Our half-track was open from the front to the back so everyone was all bundled up, sitting still, and freezing. Before departing someone discovered that the truck was carrying halves of slaughtered pigs. After we entered the countryside we drove close to the open back of their truck and one of our crewmen clambered out over the hood and leapt lightly into the bed. He selected half a pig, hauled it out, and passed it back to two others. The carcass was frozen stiff and we hid it in the back under a blanket. Without stopping, our little caravan parted in the next village to their waves of thanks and our grinning nods of acknowledgement.

Although the enemy was just 100 to 150 yards from the house beside our new gun position, the Russians weren't bothering us so we decided to relax for the evening. Between Christmas and New Year we accumulated a lot of vodka from our special rations. We were storing nearly 15 gallons of alcohol in water cans. We also had plenty of artificial honey which was hard as a brick. We were sitting in the house when I had the idea of melting the honey on my cooking stove until it was liquid. Afterwards, I took the hot honey outside and placed it in the snow to cool off, then stirred in the vodka. I was adding so much vodka that we were beginning to really like the taste of it.

I returned from one of my visits outside to discover that Ludwig Kluge had taken my place in front of a blacked-out window. I didn't comment on it because Ludwig and I were close friends and had been together ever since we had first met while training at Herford.

We were all feeling pretty good, and in the candlelight that flickered over the faces gathered inside, we began comparing our degustatory skills. All of a sudden a sniper's tracer bullet ripped through the window opening, striking the ceiling. Everybody jumped up looking for pliers or some other tool to pull the thing from where it had lodged in a wooden rafter before it caught fire. Ludwig remained seated the whole time so when I came back I asked him what was the matter?

"I think that I am wounded," he said. I opened his shirt and sure enough, I discovered the bullet had entered his back, angled down towards the ground, and ricocheted up to the ceiling. He had unwittingly exchanged places and the risks that went with it.

We took Ludwig to our field hospital and the company physician who was considered a specialist in belly shots which were most often fatal. After Ludwig's operation we were informed that the bullet had pierced his intestines 25 times. When we visited him, he was in a special ward for gut wounds under the watchful eye of a medic. In this ward, an orderly was always present to make sure that after an operation no one had anything to drink for seven days to allow the intestines time to start healing. To help stave off the feeling of thirst, the orderly placed damp sponges in the patients' mouths.

Three to four days later there was an emergency in another ward and the orderly left to lend a hand. After he departed Ludwig drank the contents of his warming bottle and two days later he was dead. It was the most difficult and memorable event of my second, and last, winter on the Eastern *HKL*.

Münster, Germany, 1943. Averbeck during first 21-day furlough from the Russian front.

Dorogobuzh, Russia, summer 1943, Averbeck, right.

Dorogobuzh, Russia, summer 1943, card game with Averbeck, right.

Averbeck, Dorogobuzh, Russia, summer 1943.

Bryansk, Russia, summer 1943. In action against Russian T-34s and infantry.

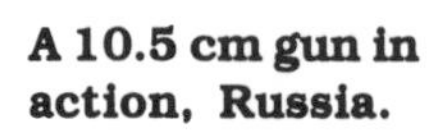

A 10.5 cm gun in action, Russia.

A 7.5 antitank gun in action, Russia.

CHAPTER IV

1944
The Polotsk Lowlands

WE fought in the region of the *Bolvastellung* through January 1944 when we moved north past Orsha and Mogilev to Vitebsk in the Polotsk Lowlands. In that region, little meadows surrounded the villages dotting the forest that stretched from horizon to horizon. The countryside provided a very good hiding place for partisans. In part this was because it was too large an area to effectively occupy, and in part this was because tanks were unable to operate in the huge lowland forests and marshy terrain.

When we reached Vitebsk we learned that we were being sent into an area where the Russian regular army and partisans had been holding out since 1941. This force had a peculiar origin. When the German army was advancing to the east in 1941 and 1942, they bypassed these huge forests and left inside whomever was in there. When we were retreating in 1943 and 1944 the regular army forces to our front and semi-irregular forces to our rear posed a real danger.

In the spring of 1944 German headquarters ordered us to help clean out the partisans inhabiting the area around the city of Lepel, between Borosof, Begomy, Seno, and Vitebsk. Two divisions surrounded the zone while our division split the encircled countryside into two smaller circles. The whole operation lasted about fourteen days.

It is hard when you have to fight against partisans. During the day when you see them working in the fields they are in civilian clothes. During the night they were shooting at you. And they didn't stop. Kids of 10 and 12 years old were carrying ammunition; girls

15 to 16 years old carried ammunition, rifles, machine pistols, and hand grenades. If you fight against another uniform, another soldier, there are certain rules both sides observe. Civilians didn't observe any rule and the fighting was sometimes very vicious. Women and men would fight to the last and never give in. Alongside the partisans we also found numerous Russian regular soldiers that had been in hiding since 1941.

After our battles to split the Lepel area were over, we were stationed in a village between the two zones we had created. Our company had two antitank guns in the village supporting the infantry who were in front of us with little short-barreled 50 mm cannons of the type pulled around by two men.

One evening, after two days there, we shot a pig foraging near our gun. Stray livestock were common in battle areas. Fresh meat was always in short supply and a first-come, first-serve attitude prevailed when encountering your next meal. After cleaning the animal we brought it back to the home where we were staying and presented the internal organs to the housewife.

Her husband hung the pig on the inside of the door letting into the narrow lean-to attached to their one room house. This entry area served to protect chickens or other farm animals, store grains and tools. In the next room was the living and eating area, and *prischko* with its sleeping platform.

We were talking amongst ourselves in the main room when an unearthly high-pitched wail raised the hair on our necks. We rushed out to the entryway and there saw the husband laying dead, his wife crying and swaying over him. A stray bullet had passed through the door and the pig killing her husband while he was butchering the carcass.

The front line was close by and the sound of gunfire was commonplace. But while we had been inside the shooting had become heavier and heavier on the outskirts of the village. I grabbed my helmet and ran to our gun that was located between two nearby houses facing an open field. I was preparing to support my gun crew with our MG34, when all of a sudden our infantry were trotting past us saying that the Russians were coming on horses. Our sergeant hadn't received any order to leave so we stayed put. Still, we didn't know from what direction the attack would come.

Behind us, in the middle of the village road there was a well surrounded by a waist-high wooden skirt designed to keep people and animals from falling in. I grabbed my machine gun and took a position behind the well boards facing the direction from where the infantry had come. I didn't have long to wait in the gathering darkness.

At first all I heard was the drumming thunder of horses' hooves coming by the hundreds. And then I saw them. Luckily for us the temperamental MG34 worked perfectly that night and when they were within range I emptied almost five boxes of ammunition. When the village across the field from us caught fire it silhouetted the attackers. All that came by me were riderless horses.

The battle was over as suddenly as it had erupted. The burning houses cast an eerie glow over a field littered with dark forms. Our sergeant checked our positions and more ammo was distributed. Occasional rifle shots punctuated the stillness. Horses milled about snorting. We passed the night in darkness and no one moved until dawn.

Later estimates placed the partisans at over 3,000 individuals who were trying to cut between the divide we had forced across the encircled area.

My sergeant nominated me for the Iron Cross first class. An Iron Cross was recommended for anyone demonstrating outstanding bravery in action, and were awarded in two classes dependent upon the merit of the deed. An appointment for the Iron Cross first class automatically included the second class.

At that time a corporal from a different unit was with us to gain fighting experience. On the night of the attack he was stationed on another gun and was out of position to have been of any help in the fight. However, at some time in the past he had received the Iron Cross second class and our company chief awarded him the first class even though he hardly saw any action that night. The corporal was an ongoing officer, his next step was lieutenant.

In my experience there were few—if any—internal promotions. When corporal or sergeant openings occurred replacements were seldom sought from within the ranks. Instead, someone was transferred in from companies behind the front lines. In this way aspiring professionals could fulfill all of the requirements of an officer. The experienced man in the field was almost always overlooked, and leadership sometimes suffered as a result.

We captured quite a few horses that evening and I shot some to relieve them of their agony. I had always liked horses, although I had never owned one. My earliest experience was with the baker's horse. No one knew how I managed it, but when I was about four years old I got out of the house one evening and into the baker's stable. Early the next morning, around 5 A.M., the baker was drawn from his work by the restless noises of his old mare. He discovered her snorting and shuffling in the stall with me firmly seated on her back. I remember less about that than what happened when I was taken home to my frantic, frightened mother.

I didn't know anything about horses and I was unaware that the one I kept, the only horse within reach with a saddle, was asthmatic. Each time I put him into a gallop he would start a coarse, deep wheezing. Even worse, when we came to a creek or other obstacle he would not jump over it. Instead, he would quickly stiffen his legs and stop. He nearly sent me over his head a number of times. At such moments, I dismounted and pulled him along by his bridle, walking him through, guiding him over, or around an obstacle.

I never experienced so much artillery fire as during that April after we finished the Vitebsk action. For the first time I also saw waves of Russian aircraft. In all the months before we rarely saw any multi-engine Russian bombers. We knew of their existence, it was just that prior to this time they had rarely operated in our area.

There was not much dread of tanks during intensive bombardments so our company was placed farther back, just at the limit of the Russian artillery. If the enemy broke through we could easily move to stop them. We discussed the bombardment with officers who were World War I veterans, men that had really suffered in the trenches of France. They unanimously agreed that this was much worse than anything they had ever experienced. I really felt sorry for the men who took the brunt of it because the blanket artillery barrages were always followed by massive infantry attacks. Still, we didn't lose any ground and even took large numbers of prisoners.

Two fellows in our company who spoke fluent Russian tried to speak to the prisoners and discovered they didn't understand a word of what they were saying. The prisoners explained that they were *Polska* and showed us their Bibles. We never saw a Bible on a Russian, but the Poles were carrying them. These men were former Soviet prisoners of war and civilians the Russians had taken from Poland, armed, and thrown in to fight against us. In all, we encountered two to three divisions of Polish soldiers.

I rode my horse to our next position. After we reached our destination the sergeant needed to notify our company leader that we had arrived safely and were ready for action. I was assigned the task of reporting back despite the late afternoon hour and the fact that the area was new to all of us.

I left hoping to stay with the company that night and return the following morning. However, after I reported, I was presented with an urgent dispatch for our sergeant indicating that we had to change locations first thing the next morning. So despite the distance, I set off alone into the darkness.

When I passed our last sentry I had a Russian machine pistol with a drum magazine hanging right in front of me and I had both hands on it. I let the horse choose his own route.

The road was little more than a fire break cut through the trees. It was absolutely dark with not even a moon. In the little strip of sky above me I could see stars and to the right and left the black jagged edges of the forest. Small bands of partisans had been encountered throughout the area and I admit that I was uneasy doing this alone.

My horse was slowly making his way when he shuddered, made a jump, and broke into a gallop. I don't know what scared him, I was just amazed I was still in the saddle. The excitement caught me off guard and despite the cool night air I broke out in a sweat. My horse was also sweating and wheezing noisily by the time we arrived. I brought the dispatch to the sergeant and found that it was some time before the excitement generated by the ride subsided enough for me to rest.

Rapid changes are peculiar to the military. Our initial relocation had been for nothing. The next morning we returned over the same route I had ridden twice the night before. Our two half-tracks pulling guns were ahead of me and another crewman who had also captured a horse. We were trotting along talking between ourselves when the sergeant, who was riding in the first half-track, suddenly stood and yelled back that there were two partisans with guns on the road ahead. The men disappeared into the forest before anyone could get their rifle into shooting position. The two of us rode up to where they had been spotted and turned our horses into the trees. The thick undergrowth made riding difficult so we dismounted and followed their path into the woods. We went as far as we could and when the signs stopped we were forced to give up the chase and return to the road. I believe my horse may have experienced something similar when he was spooked into a gallop the previous night.

After several days of travel we came into a village where an artillery unit had a small herd of horses sheltering in a stable. It was night and sentries were posted to the front and sides of the barn. I approached one of the guards and asked if I could put my horse inside. I was hoping to find fodder in there and sure enough, after being allowed to pass, I found everything he needed.

The next morning at daybreak it was so foggy you could barely see the ground in front of you. I went to collect my horse and there beside him was a beautiful animal, gray with black markings. Without hesitation, or even a quick good-bye to my asthmatic transport, I put my saddle on the new horse and led him over to the door. I paused before leaving and waited for the guard to go by. I passed the doorway, climbed onto his back, and trotted triumphantly out to the road where everyone was going into formation.

Our company headquarters was withdrawing to a different village and we had to arrive the same day as they did. Our half-tracks took off and because it was a good road they were able to travel rapidly. My friend and I put our horses into a trot at the rear of the group, behind the vehicles which were soon lost in the fog. We had a good three-hour ride to reach our destination and I was happy that before long the fog gave way to the low clouds of a grey somber morning.

On our way there was another village about 300 yards off the main road and in the early light we saw a lot of excited activity. We could see several horses in a pasture and someone with a team. Suddenly we heard shouts from several soldiers gesturing in our direction.

It didn't take a second to realize that the two soldiers saddling up on big German work horses had recognized the mount I was riding. We started galloping but the two quickly caught up with us in no time. Before they had stopped one yelled, "You stole that horse!"

"No, I didn't steal this horse," I replied playing dumb.

The one who had yelled dismounted, came around to my side, and lifting the front hoof of my horse said, "You see there is a number burnt into it." I couldn't deny it, the number of a battery from an artillery regiment was there before me.

"You need to come back with us," he said curtly.

The four of us rode back to the village where we were met by the driver of the team that had been one of those yelling and pointing at us. This one was really angry. He immediately came right over and started accusing me of stealing the gray the previous night and leaving a bony, wheezing nag in its place.

I protested that not being a horseman I had no idea how to tell one horse from another. All horses looked alike to me, I pretended, especially in the fog and the darkness of a stable.

I insisted on playing really stupid and it worked. I was told to take my saddle and get lost. They hadn't said what they had done with my horse and I didn't think that it was the best time to be asking. We left the group, my friend on his horse and me with my saddle over my shoulder. I carried that thing for several miles before we reached our company where we were met with laughter. I kept the saddle for a while but could never replace my horse.

Towards the end of April we were camped in a small village and walking down the road were hundreds of civilians trying to escape the advancing Soviet forces. Some drove horse-drawn buggies and carts, many were on foot. After a while the column stopped, left the road and bedded down for the night—prepared to march all the next day.

A friend and I walked down the road and looked the people over. An old man approached us and to our surprise he spoke a little German. He explained that during WW I he had been taken prisoner and put to work for a merchant delivering coal to households in Cologne. His two granddaughters were with him. We understood that he wanted to take them as far west as possible. He had told the girls that in the Europe outside of Russia, people were generally well dressed. He said his granddaughters didn't believe that women wore silky stockings and possessed more than one dress and shoes. He asked us if we had pictures of our families and if we would mind showing them to his granddaughters. Naturally we obliged. We sat down with them and showed photos of our families and girlfriends. The young girls were genuinely interested and asked us questions through their grandfather. They really were surprised and they finally admitted that they hadn't believed their grandfather and had thought that he was just telling stories, as grandparents are sometimes accustomed to do. They were happy to learn what he had been saying was true and perhaps it made their journey less difficult.

In May 1944 I received a letter from my father saying that he was about to go on leave. We had our last furlough together, and when I received his letter I requested to exchange with someone and take my leave early. The train took me from Poltsk, to Vilnius (Vilya), to Konigsberg. At Konigsberg I had a couple of hours stop over. I was deloused, given a health check and received another 20 pound package of flour, sugar, fat and oil.

From Konigsberg I continued on to Berlin, Hannover, and Münster. It was during my last furlough from the Eastern Front in mid-May 1944 that my mother persuaded me to see a doctor for my gastritis.

I was still in the hospital when the Americans and their allies invaded Normandy. A political officer who visited us regularly was always putting everything in glory, describing how we would beat the American and British forces. He used a map to demonstrate how a pincer movement would cut them all off before they could move inland. The pincer action never materialized, and we knew that the end of the war was only a matter of time.

At first everyone in my ward was apprehensive to talk about the political officer's ideas because nobody knew their fellow patient. After several weeks had passed we developed enough mutual trust to talk frankly about fighting for a lost cause. We didn't talk to our officers that way, but in the evenings we soldiers lying in our hospital beds, listening to the radio, were well aware of the situation.

I left the hospital towards the end of June 1944 with ten days medical furlough and learned that the *95. Infanterie Division* had been overrun and destroyed. Afterwards, I was sent back to my original training post at Herford.

In May when I had left on furlough, we were still in the vicinity of Uschatsch near Minsk and when I left the hospital the Russians were on the border of East Prussia edging on the Baltic Sea.

When I had left the company the *HKL* was really peaceful. Certainly, at the center and in the south the Russians were pushing and regaining a lot of their country. But in our area around Vitebsk, in the northern part of Army Group Center, it was quiet at that time. In late June, all hell broke loose when the Russians staged their last great summer offensive and their largest northern operation to date. I would later learn that the roughly 50 German infantry divisions in our zone were overrun by 146 Soviet infantry divisions and 53 armored units. According to the same newspaper and Red Cross accounts, Vitebsk became a prison camp where the approximately 150,000 Germans who were gathered there died at the rate of between forty and fifty each day.

I didn't know immediately how many guys disappeared. Our company counted between 120 and 128 men. Usually a company was 200 men, although for that time we were in full strength. At Herford I met a handful of men from the 95th and the stories I heard there were really horrific. We lost 80 percent of our unit; few were thought to have made it into P.O.W. camps.

A company of six guns was a fighting unit but then you also had need of support. So, in addition to the 36 men manning the guns there was the tailor, the shoemaker, the barber, the cooks, the mechanics, and the men from ordnance. Also, almost every unit had some kind of civilian help we referred to as *Hiwis* or more properly *Hilfefreiwillige*. These people were not pressed into this service. They performed their tasks voluntarily. Money didn't mean anything to them, but the food and protection that they were receiving did. Our company had a couple of Russian women working in the kitchen.

We kept a small herd of horses for use with our carts. Although we were mechanized the horses and carts were often the most reliable means of transportation. One of the Russian girls and one of our stablemen, responsible for watching over the horses and feeding them, were close friends.

When the Soviets started their offensive in the north and succeeded in breaking through our front lines there was general chaos. When the Russians encircled the unit in mid-1944 the chaos became a desperate bid for individual survival and it was at this time the Russian girl and our stableman escaped on horseback. Whenever approaching a village the girl always rode ahead to make sure that no Russian soldiers or partisans were occupying the site. If the village was already occupied they would make a big detour around the area. These two rode bareback for two weeks before they rejoined the German lines.

Many were killed; a few were taken prisoner as was the case with our company barber. Our barber told me the Russians broke through just after I left and from that time on, the company was hightailing it for the German border. He also told me that he was alive only because one of the Russian officers spoke German. The officer ordered our barber to put down his weapon and surrender. The others saw this as an opportunity to kill him until the officer intervened and ordered him to be taken back under escort behind the front lines, then to the hinterland.

Each German prisoner of war was brought before a Peoples' Tribunal. These trials were not for cruelty to civilians nor for war crimes. Our barber, for example, was asked if he ever stole anything from the Russian people?

"No," he replied.

Then they came out with this question: "Did you ever eat potatoes?"

"Yes."

"Where did you get the potatoes?"

"I don't know."

The tribunal officers maintained that these were Russian potatoes. And, indeed, they most likely were Russian potatoes. We always supplemented our rations with whatever was at hand.

The panel declared that the barber had eaten potatoes stolen from the Russian people and for this he was sentenced to 30 years of hard labor. I only learned of his story in 1948. When he was released he was so near death, it was years before he was once again back to near normal health.

After the war I stayed in contact with a few men yet no one was ever able to tell me that more came back from the Russian camps. When I think of our division being overrun, I have never been able to get beyond the memory of the Russians calling to us on loudspeakers saying that they would eventually get us, because indeed they had.

While at Herford I encountered our former company clerk. When I met him he said, "What are you doing? You aren't a simple private or *Gefreiter*, you're the next rank higher, an *Obergefreiter*. I know. I handled all your papers and saw that they were signed." This confirmed what had been contained in the telegram sent to my mother while I was hospitalized. When I didn't immediately return to the front, I was listed as missing in action. The telegram had referred to *Obergefreiter* Averbeck.

With the higher rank I was paid monthly, not every ten days. As a soldier you received one *Reichmark* per day. If you were in combat your pay was doubled. Hence, if you were a private you received 20 *Reichmarks* every ten days. When you were an *Obergefreiter* you received 136 *Reichmarks* per month plus your combat pay of one *Reichmark* per day. I should have been receiving over 160 *Reichmarks* per month. Our clerk was in the process of preparing a formal written statement so that I could obtain the higher grade and pay rate when he was transferred out of Herford. He didn't have time to complete it.

When I had returned home in May, my girlfriend and I were formally engaged. The first Sunday after my assignment to Herford she came out to spend the day with me. It was a nice afternoon and we were sitting and talking at an empty outdoor restaurant when she said to me, "Close your eyes."

I squeezed my eyes shut and I felt her fingers undo one button on my soldier's blouse. I knew she was putting something on me, I was just unsure what it was. When she told me to open my eyes again I saw my Iron Cross. I was very surprised and then she gave me the certificate for it signed by Major General Michaelis. For whatever reason, I had not received my Iron Cross during an awards' ceremony with my company. Instead, it was sent to my girlfriend's home. I'm sure that there are few of us from that time, who had the pleasure of their girlfriend presenting them their medal.

I stayed at Herford for a while in what was called a *marsch* company. Everyone was literally awaiting their marching orders. One afternoon 400 guys were present and the next day only five were left. For a while I had a good thing going there.

Uschatsk, Russia, April 1944. Russian civilians heading west.

Uschatsk, Russia, April 1944. Averbeck on horse captured at Lepel.

Averbeck after being wounded, Elend, Harz Mountains, Germany, January 1945.

Averbeck's Soldbuch, identification tag, and Catholic song book.

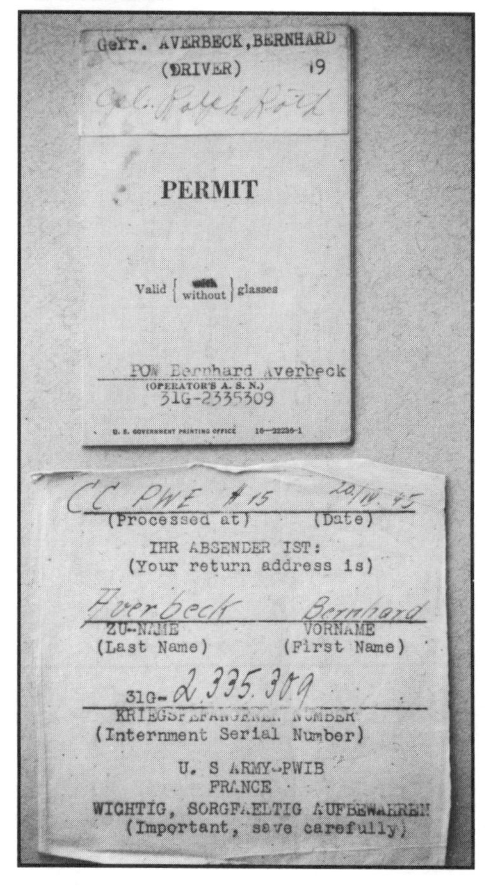

Gefr. AVERBECK, BERNHARD
(DRIVER) 19
Cpl. Ralph Roth

PERMIT

Valid { ~~with~~ without } glasses

POW Bernhard Averbeck
(OPERATOR'S A. S. N.)
31G-2335309

U. S. GOVERNMENT PRINTING OFFICE 16—22236-1

CC PWE #15 20/IV. 45
(Processed at) (Date)
IHR ABSENDER IST:
(Your return address is)

Averbeck Bernhard
ZU-NAME VORNAME
(Last Name) (First Name)

31G- 2.335.309
KRIEGSGEFANGENEN NUMBER
(Internment Serial Number)

U. S ARMY-PWIB
FRANCE
WICHTIG, SORGFAELTIG AUFBEWAHREN
(Important, save carefully)

Averbeck's POW driving permit, issued by Corporal Ralph Roth.

Averbeck's award letters, Iron Cross second class, and identification tag.

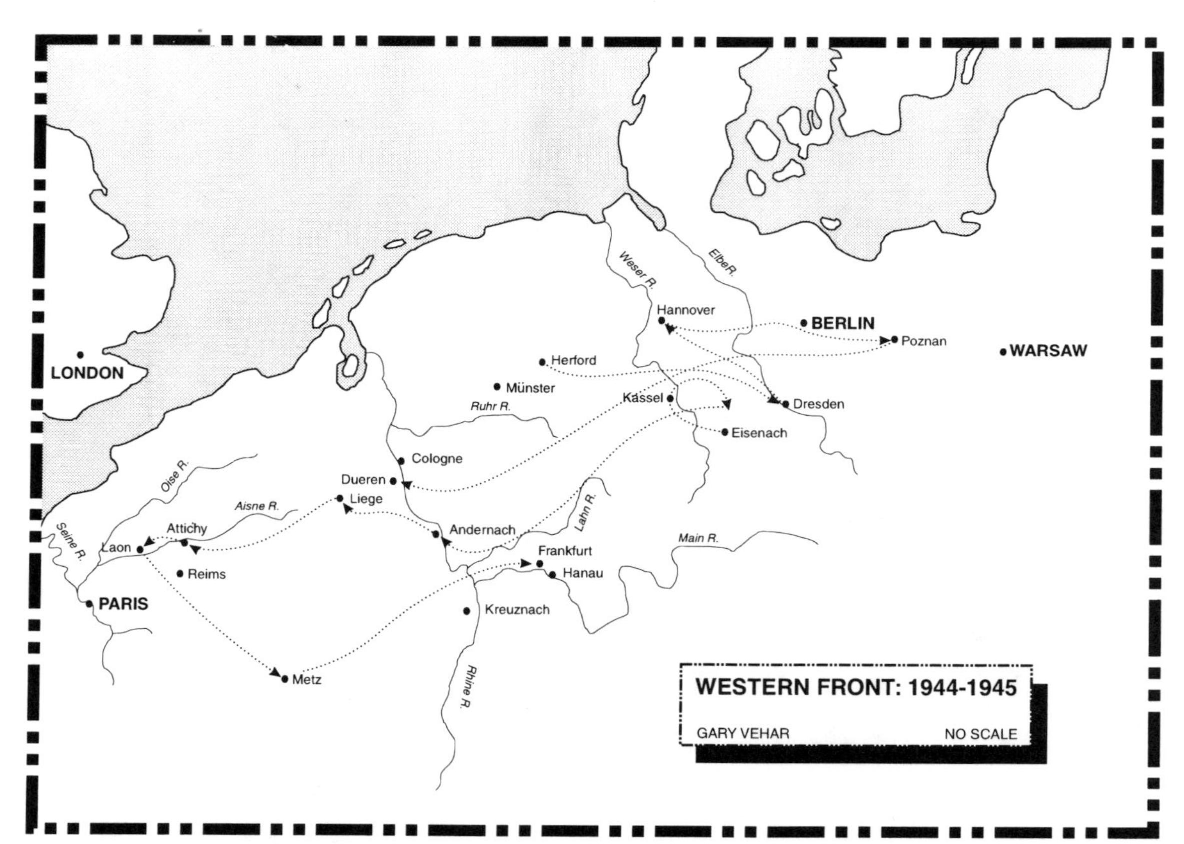

Bernhard Averbeck's movements on the Western Front, 1944–1945.

CHAPTER V

1944
Die Westliche HKL

EVERY morning the company assembled before the master sergeant in typical garrison formation. He carried a thick duty book and while he had everyone mustered he issued our work assignments. One morning he asked for any electricians among us to step out of line and to the left. Right away I stepped forward. Afterwards he came to me and asked, "Do you know anything about putting up antennas?"

I had always found it helpful to volunteer and so I always knew everything. One of my principles was that whenever a volunteer was needed I was always available. I never, ever, went wrong with that, and for myself, it was always for the better. I had made two friends in the company so I told the master sergeant that I needed the help of at least two others. On my recommendation, he called my two friends out of line as well.

Our 1st lieutenant lived in the barracks and he wanted an antenna for his radio. I told him I could do this, but I needed to locate copper wire and other materials. He gave us permission to go to town and buy whatever was required. We gathered the materials together on the first day, although "officially," it took about four afternoons to obtain everything. Every time we returned to base I recounted how the merchant assured me that maybe tomorrow the goods would be available.

My mother had sent me some ration cards for five grams of fat or 10 grams of butter, the 25-gram meat, and the 100-gram bread. While off base, the three of us ate at Herford's *Soldatenheim* using our ration cards. The *Soldatenheim* provided inexpensive fare—less expensive than a regular restaurant—and this allowed me to stretch out my ration allowances. After eating we would go to a movie and during four days we generally had a good time.

When we returned from town on the afternoon of the fourth day I proudly announced that we had acquired everything and could begin erecting the antenna. My dental experience as a recruit had not been for nothing. In the meanwhile, British bombers had damaged a Herford bank.

The bank manager was the father of the 1st lieutenant's girlfriend and he needed his bank's electrical wiring repaired. After I finished the antenna he asked if we would mind going over to the bank and helping out. I was no longer eager to go back to the Eastern Front. I was eager when I was seventeen but after two years there it was a different story. My friends and I were more than ready to be of service at the bank where we were treated as civilian employees and paid electrician wages. This was a pleasing addition to our more modest military pay. We made that job last four weeks.

On July 20 we returned from town and, as we passed the gate, the sentries called us into the guardhouse. We were told that beginning today everyone had to give the Party salute. Why? we asked. They explained to us that an attempt had been made to assassinate Hitler. It was the first that we had heard of it.

We always greeted officers with the standard military salute. When we changed over to the Party salute not everyone complied. Quite a few older officers would not salute with their arm upraised and insisted acknowledging one another with the traditional military salute given with the right arm bent so that the extended fingers touched the forehead.

On Saturdays there was little activity in a company except for cleaning your room or personal equipment. By noon we could go to town until Sunday night. After the attempt on Hitler's life, Himmler took over all the reserves in Germany and set Saturdays aside for field exercises. Thanks to our bank job, my two friends and I were excused to work in town on Saturdays—even though on weekends there was no work at the bank. We had a swell time.

One day the whole camp was ordered to Verona, Italy. I was standing in an inspection line with the rest of the men listening to a farewell speech being given by some officers when the master sergeant saw me and called out, "Averbeck, what are you doing there?"

"I'm going to Verona," I replied.

"No you don't. Out! Out!"

"I have drawn all my equipment and weapons," I protested.

"Bring it back!"

From then on I was his valet. He had a room in the barracks but he lived in town. When he came in the morning he changed his uniform and his boots and I brought his daily ration to his quarters. This generally consisted of bread and butter with marmalade and some sausage. He never ate it, I did. For me it was something extra and greatly appreciated. I occupied myself with cleaning his uniform, boots, and other gear, and even babysat his son.

In late September 1944, he could do no more. I was sent from Herford to the city of Spremberg on the Spree River, 45 miles northeast of Dresden. There I learned that I was a member of a new unit destined for the Eastern Front in Poland. From Spremberg I traveled to a huge, live ammunition training site for tankers, artillerymen, and antitank crews located in the region of Luneberger Heide, between the towns of Hamburg and Ulzen in the north, and Hannover and Celle in the south.

It was there, while training for my new unit, that I was introduced to the 88 mm antitank gun. The 88 was really a superb weapon. There were two models, the first had a gun undercarriage like a cross and a barrel at least four feet off the ground. The second had the old-fashioned undercarriage that split so the gun looked like an inverted Y. Both guns had oversized barrels. And those with the old-fashioned undercarriage had barrels fabricated from two lengths of tubing. When we fired the two-part barrel gun, one-half of the tube followed the projectile as it disappeared into the distance. Our major declined to accept that model and instead requested the one with the undercarriage like a cross.

When we assembled in Luneberger Heide I encountered my old company officer from Russia. He had been the first—1st lieutenant to lead our company. In the summer of 1942 during our offensive across the Tim River he was wounded and sent back to Germany. Now he was a major.

We were on parade when he saw me standing in line. He came right to me and asked how long I had stayed with the 195th and everything that had happened. He wanted me in his headquarters staff, but I declined, explaining that I would rather be in the field.

At Luneberger Heide we were restricted to firing only enough rounds to familiarize ourselves with the 88's range finder and breech mechanism. After our training was completed in September, we were sent to Poznan, Poland. Poznan, situated between Berlin to the west and Warsaw to the east, had been declared a *Festung*, a fortress city. We traveled there by train and upon our arrival we received three ton half-tracks and 88s with which we could really train.

One afternoon in the fog and drizzle I had an opportunity to watch one of our *Hornisse*, the Hornet, 88 mm self-propelled antitank cannons at work. *Hornisses* were open-topped armored vehicles with armor plating surrounding the gun deck. The crew had been issued the same range finder used by antiaircraft batteries. It was incredibly accurate.

The front line was 800 yards from our position and 1200 yards beyond Russian tanks were idling in their forward assembly areas. As I watched through my field glasses the *Hornisse* cut loose on two T-34s destroying both of them. It was like observing an ant hill being stirred up with a stick. The Russian tankers had thought that they were out of range and they had no idea what had hit them.

At the beginning of October I was appointed gun leader. We marched, drilled, cleaned our weapons, and did any and every thing to keep busy. The rainy fall weather, that is so characteristic of the north, was depressing and miserable.

One night I was in charge of the 24-hour duty watch that in my case stretched from 6 o'clock to 6 o'clock the next day. Whoever was in charge was responsible for the continual surveying of all the guard posts.

Our company officer was a 1st lieutenant who had never been in combat. Prior to my watch, he gave an order that all on-duty gun leaders and their guards were not allowed to remove their shoes for the duration of their 24-hour watch. I put my guards into position, then made my rounds checking that no one fell asleep. The whole day I was in the field, in the rain, and my boots were soaked. After making several rounds I entered a little hut with an oven. I wrung out my socks and placed my boots near the stove. I felt miserable, the October weather in the east is always wet but this seemed unrelenting. Just as I finished arranging my footwear the 1st lieutenant came in. I jumped up, called everyone to attention and reported to him. He angrily claimed that in one of the ammo bunkers he had found one of my guards using a flashlight to read a letter. Because the guard hadn't heard him coming he hadn't challenged him with the password and so he was in deep shit, and so was I when he saw my barefeet. Convinced that I was the source of his problems he tore into me, concluding that tomorrow I was to report to his office as soon as I was off duty.

Near the end of my watch I spoke to my other superiors and first sergeant. They assured me that it would all come to nothing. They reasoned that the lieutenant wanted to demonstrate that he merited his commission, to say that he had been on the front line and that he maintained discipline. They all said that there was really nothing to worry about.

At 6:30 I reported to his office and he ordered me locked up for seven days alongside the guard who had been reading the letter. I felt as if someone had hit me with a sledge hammer. I was shocked. All my papers had been processed so that I could become a non-commissioned officer. With the seven days' detention I lost everything. I returned to my quarters where my friends urged me to let the major know what had happened. Not wanting to take advantage of our friendship I accepted the injustice as it was.

Three days later I was ordered to the office. The soldier who had been reading was already there. Before we were marched off under guard to a Polish jail cell, I was instructed to remove my belt, and even my suspenders. When we arrived, the 1st lieutenant was waiting outside the jail. He ordered the soldier on guard to search us for any forbidden materials. Prior to leaving the barracks my sergeant gave me a big sausage, tobacco, and cigarettes. I know the guard felt the hidden sausage and cigarettes, but he didn't say anything.

It so happened that the jailer was Polish and my cell mate spoke Polish. We befriended the jailer who in turn kept a nice fire in the oven and even brought us things to eat. All in all we were cozy, warm and dry. It was far better than being wet, cold, and in the field with the company. At the end of the second afternoon our sergeant visited long enough to say come with him, "We're moving west."

The following day we left for Cologne, then continued on to Dueren and the Rhine River where we stopped opposite the American Ninth Army. Poznan's lead-colored sky and rain were left behind.

Our company was attached to a *Heeresgruppe* Heavy Antitank unit. When we first arrived in Dueren it was still a beautiful town, practically untouched by the war, and we were billeted in private homes, just like in Russia. This didn't last long. On the second day the gun companies left town and took up positions on the outskirts of the city.

I was still a gun leader. There were guys with ranks higher than I had but they were all without experience. I chose a spot beside an antiaircraft (AA) battery in the shadow of an old factory. We dug in our gun and prepared foxholes. We didn't have any idea from where to expect an American attack, or even if they would attack through the city.

The third day dawned clear. After lunch the air alarms sounded and minutes later American B-17s bombed Dueren. As I watched V-shaped formations filled the air first with the sonorous rumble of their engines and then the whistle and crash of bomb after exploding bomb. All of the antiaircraft batteries around the city were shooting at them. Dark puffs of exploding antiaircraft fire mottled the blue sky. I was sitting in my foxhole, watching and listening to the sound of airplane engines punctuated by the AA fire when suddenly one of our bursts tore into a dark-colored bomber. Our gunners had hit the lead plane in a group of three passing overhead. The exploding craft burst into a hot ball of fire, ripped into the two other planes and caused them to explode as well.

I was staring up at the scene trying to take it all in when I felt like someone struck me with a 200 pound sack of cement. The shock wave generated by the explosion, a gust of hot formless air, snatched the breath from my lungs while roughly shoving me backwards into my foxhole. Debris of all sizes was falling everywhere around us. There were no white parachutes among the remnants of the falling crafts.

The bombardment flattened the city. The dust had not even settled when two young girls suddenly appeared at our gun. Homeless and frightened they attached themselves to me and I found it was impossible to persuade them to leave. After some searching, I was able to get a local married couple to take them into their care.

After the airstrike we picked up and moved even farther into the countryside, in this case a barnyard. I instructed my crew on how to use a pile of cow dung to camouflage our gun. The following day we had an inspection and the major, along with my company leader and others, nearly walked right by us. The major attributed the successfulness of the camouflage to me exclusively, saying that it was the result of my extensive practical knowledge gained on the Eastern Front. It was obvious that the major's hearty congratulation stung my company leader who was without any practice tempered by front line know-how. The major was not incorrect, I always acted upon first-hand experience whereas the lieutenant always acted by the book. After the visiting officers had departed my 1st lieutenant returned and rudely reminded me that I had five more days of jail time to serve.

In the aftermath of the American bombardment Dueren was a rubble field. Headquarters had parked their vehicles beside the same houses where their staff was being quartered and the walls of crumbling houses had nearly buried them both. For the next five days I was assigned to a punishment detail ordered to clear away the debris from the trucks and cars.

Seven of us gathered at headquarters and because I was the oldest in rank I went in to report. While I was speaking the major appeared in the doorway of his office and asked, "Averbeck, what are you doing here?" He invited me into his office and after the door was shut I told him everything. There was nothing he could do. I had been punished and my promotion had been retracted. However, he did request that I make a full written report. Shortly after, we were constantly on the move and I was unable to finish the statement that I was preparing.

We were required to dig out one vehicle per day. No one was supervising us, so before getting started we explored the ruins of nearby homes and discovered numerous wine cellars. The wine was an unexpected windfall. When we started on our first vehicle, we stopped a heavy truck passing through town and had the driver pull us out in exchange for a couple of bottles. The lieutenant was expecting us to extract the vehicles by hand but using our barter system we finished our quota in two hours. After that we got out of sight and began tasting all different kinds of wine, some 20 to 30 years old. We were not connoisseurs and we were drinking it like lemonade.

Each night, after reporting back to headquarters, we locked ourselves inside a private garage. The door locked from the inside; there wasn't any guard. We had our rations, a hand-cranked gramaphone with records, and a couple cases of wine. All of us started drinking that night and I wasn't sober for the next four days. The greatest danger was when I checked in.

On the second evening I walked into the office to report. I had just started speaking when the sergeant behind the desk said, "You smell funny."

"Well", I answered, "you know with all the dust and rubble . . . ," but before I could finish he came around his desk and interrupted me saying, "That's not dust, that's alcohol."

I was losing a fight against what felt like an uncontrollable grin when I heard myself admitting that indeed it was and would he care to accept a few bottles? The exchange worked, and afterwards he never asked about anything.

In the beginning of December, we went into new positions deeper in the surrounding countryside. My gun was ordered to the outskirts of a little single street village approximately 13 yards from the first house. I set about locating us in the same way we had always done in Russia. The barrel of our 88 was nearly four feet off the ground. For camouflage we dug out the soil until we had a U-shaped hole about thigh deep that we could back our 88 into. We had a clear field of fire and we were well hidden. The hole provided us with maximum protection and the gun a nearly flat trajectory that maximized the power of it penetration. Afterwards we moved into the cellar of the first house.

On December 16 we started our last major offensive against the Americans and their allies in the west. The sky was overcast that day so when we heard the sound of airplanes it drew us from our cellar. At first we thought that the Americans must have started something. When I checked my compass I realized these planes were flying east to west so they must be German. I took out my field glasses and tried to get a better view. The craft were flying just at the limit of the overcast and for the most part were veiled by the clouds. Every once in a while one or two dipped out of the cloud cover and judging by the noise of the engines, there must have been hundreds in the air.

That was our last hurrah on the Western Front. Two days later I got an order to get ready to move out for Belgium. I had the men load everything and then we returned to our cellar to wait. The next morning as we were getting ready to trailer the gun behind our three ton half-track an American spotter plane flew overhead. I ordered everyone back into the house, and forbade any movement outside.

I was pressed for time. I had an hour and a location where I was to meet the rest of the company and we couldn't afford to be late. I waited a few minutes and then gave the order to get outside and heave the gun up onto its four wheels. We were securing it behind the half-track when the air filled with a ZZZHHH-like sound as two artillery grenades came down. The airplane hadn't left and the pilot had spotted us. The explosions were near "misses." My gunner, who was standing beside me, was hit in his left arm and leg by shrapnel. We hurried back into the cellar and while I bandaged my gunner we waited to see if there was going to be another fly-by. As it happened, these were the only projectiles that were fired. There was no damage to either the gun or half-track so we hooked the two together and headed for our rendezvous.

After we had gotten under way I was sitting in the half-track when I became aware of blood running from under my sleeve down my right wrist. At first, I thought that hurrying to secure the gun I had cut or scratched myself, but this was bleeding pretty good so I took off my jacket. When we were attacked I had been standing beside my gunner and at that moment I hadn't suspected that I had been hit. Now I discovered that I had been wounded in my right leg and my right bicep at the same time as my companion had been struck in his left side.

Upon joining the company I reported that two of us had been wounded. We were sent to see a corpsman and after a brief check they transported us back to the nearest field hospital.

When we arrived at the schoolhouse hospital those of us who were able to stand formed a long line that began beside the operating table. The blood-smeared doctors wearing rubber aprons looked just like butchers. Two of them were bent over the table. As we stood in line I could see what they were doing to the man in front, and the man behind could see everything that happened to me, and so on to the last man.

When they lifted the person in front of me off the table I stepped forward and laid down. The doctor standing at my head asked, "Do you wear false teeth?"

The moment that I uttered "No" he pressed a big wad of cotton on my nose and said, "Breath." I did and I immediately lost consciousness.

I woke up to find my right arm and chest wrapped in plaster. My arm was bent at the elbow and uncomfortably fixed in place at a 90-degree angle. A chunk of metal had been removed from my bicep. I still carry the one in my thigh.

The guy who had been standing behind me was in the same ward. He told me afterwards that the whole time they were operating I was shouting and yelling commands to my gun crew.

We were moved onto hospital trains, each car clearly marked with a red cross on a white field. The train transported us away from the front line to the center of Germany, and the resort area of Mount Brocken in the Harz Mountains. My hospital was a converted resort in the town of Elend. Waist deep snow covered the forested landscape, and everything was very peaceful and comfortable. I met my first American there. He was as young as the rest of us and occupied the bed at the end of the ward.

After I was able to walk satisfactorily, I stood by the window and with the sunlight reflecting from the snow outside I photographed myself in the dresser mirror.

I had been wounded on December 16, at the exact moment that we were to advance into Belgium. Rundstedt's offensive aimed at Liege and splitting the Allied armies failed and once again I had been spared while others of the heavy antitank unit that I had become a part of perished. On January 26, 1945, *Festung* Poznan was encircled and destroyed. By January 31, the Russians were only 40 miles from Berlin.

I was kept in the hospital from December 1944 to the beginning of February 1945. Confined to a resort-like setting over Christmas and New Year was not such a bad idea after all.

CHAPTER VI

1945
P.W.

I was released from the hospital with fourteen days' medical leave. I walked home from the train station to discover we had been bombed out. My mother had written a message on the wall for myself and my father, it read: We are alive. We are in this and this village. Just knowing that my mother and sister were alive was relief enough. I returned to the station and tried to find a train. Because it was Sunday morning even fewer trains than normal were running. When I finally caught one, I discovered I would still have to walk over thirty miles to reach my family.

We were rolling along under cloudy, low-cast skies, lulled into rest by the clicking passage of the cars over the steel rails, when double-bodied P-38 Lightnings dropped on us, strafing and bombing as they roared overhead. The train screeched to an abrupt stop. Everybody around me was yelling, their children crying while rushing for cover in the fields to either side of the cars. I noticed that white clouds were coming from the direction of the engine just as the planes made another attack, strafing along the length of the train. The locomotive was not destroyed. After the first attack the engineer had opened up all the valves and the steam billowing up gave the impression that his engine had been rendered useless. The ruse must have been successful because during the second attack the pilots went after the carriages. It was an overcast day so the pilots' sight could not have been too good and after their second pass they departed. Amazingly, none of the passengers hidden in the fields were hurt. When the engineer had built up enough steam to get under way everybody climbed back aboard. No one rested for the remainder of the trip. Most of the passengers were young mothers and children being relocated in the countryside away from the danger of aerial attack.

When I arrived at the village, I discovered that my mother and sister were lodging with a farmer. There was only the old man, his daughter-in-law and his two granddaughters. His son was in the army. The daughter-in-law was sick and unable to walk. Her two children were only four and five years old, so life on the farm was pretty hard.

In order to help keep the farm operating a French prisoner of war and a Polish girl named Marie had been assigned to work for the old man. The prisoner's name was Juhle and he went alone every night to his prison camp, and returned each morning to the farm all by himself. It was a prison camp without fences. All of the farmers around there had similar prisoners of war helping on their farms.

My aunt and uncle and their children were being housed at a neighboring farm. One day, when I visited them, I was astounded how well the two French prisoners working there spoke German. When I returned that evening to the house I asked my mother out of curiosity, how come Juhle doesn't speak German. I quickly discovered that the old man was a bastard.

My mother was raised in Liege and spoke perfect French. Shortly after their arrival she had asked Juhle why it was that he wouldn't speak a word of German. He had answered that the old man wouldn't let him or Marie eat in the kitchen with his family. Instead, they were required to eat where they prepared the pigs' food. He had no desire to learn as long as he and Marie were not allowed to eat in the house with everyone else. His response and reasoning was perfectly understandable. My mother was upset about this arrangement and told Juhle, "Wait and see."

One evening, some days after I departed, she surprised the old man while he was listening to BBC (British Broadcasting Company), London. The British were broadcasting in German every day for several hours and it was strictly forbidden to listen to any foreign broadcast. And it didn't matter where the broadcast originated, Sweden, England, or Switzerland. You were not allowed to listen to any foreign broadcast. My mother was shocked because the old man had always emphasized that he was such a good Party member. "Well," my mother declared, "now I see what kind of Party member you really are."

He begged my mother not to say anything, not knowing that to report him was the furthest thing from her mind. She seized the occasion to tell him that from now on Juhle and Marie were to eat in the main kitchen with everyone else. He readily agreed and afterwards they always ate together. Every morning Marie and Juhle milked the cows and, out of their kindness and gratitude, they always brought fresh cream to my mother.

Juhle talked openly to my mother. While I was visiting, he told her "We know that the end to the war is just a matter of weeks away and our whole camp is prepared to hide in the forest. We have built bunkers and we are planning to disappear and wait out the rest of the war." Then he came to the point, "We would like to take your son along and then you will know that he will survive the war." My mother revealed the plan to me and I declined. "I can't do that. First of all there is a company of SS close by the village and if I do not show up on the day my furlough is over, even with the extra two to three days allotted for delays in trains and destroyed roads and the like, the nearest military *Kommandantur* would be alerted." The risk was far too great. I most certainly would have lost my life and I am convinced that my mother and sister would have paid a similar price. So I took the other gamble and thought to myself that I might have a chance to come out alive anyway.

I later learned that upon the appointed day the French prisoners commandeered a truck and on the way to their forest hideout they entered a minefield. I never knew if Juhle survived. Unfortunately, the old man's son was killed just at the end of the war.

After my medical leave I reported to the town of Eisenach where I was placed into another *marsch* company. One morning, on about my tenth day there, we were ordered to assemble in formation. A group of officers began going from person to person asking their names, what sort of training they had, and where they had fought. I noticed that as they went along they picked men here and there out of the lines. When they came to me they asked my name and how long and where I had been in combat. I was also chosen although I didn't know for what I was being selected.

Everyone who had been taken out of line was ordered to report to the company office. There they informed us that we were now instructors for a noncommissioned officers' training school that was formerly located in Kolberg on the Baltic Sea. Many of the original instructors had been called up for active duty and a large number had been lost. The school had been relocated near Eisenach and they were trying to rebuild their staff.

The recruits we got were from 17 to 18 years old and had never seen combat. I was 20 years old but my experience overrode any similarity in our ages.

Because we didn't have heavy weapons with which to instruct them, the only thing I could do was drill my group in basic infantry skills and how to fire and care for a rifle and machine gun. Everyday we marched into the countryside and with our unloaded weapons you could say that we were playing war, while the real war swirled around us.

On one memorable late March afternoon our practice drills brought us to the top of a grassy height. Our rest spot was a scenic promontory dominated by the ruins of a medieval castle. We paused there to watch a passenger train on the valley floor below us departing from the Herleshausen station.

On April 1, I was to receive my rank as a noncommissioned officer. My first chance at promotion had been nullified when I was punished with seven days' lockup at Poznan. This was my second opportunity and I was really excited about it. The ceremony commemorating my commissioning and others was to be included in a torchlight ceremony beside the castle ruins on April 20th, Hitler's birthday.

Six American P-47 Thunderbolts shattered my reverie. They came out of nowhere and we instinctively threw ourselves to the dirt. We were so high that we were able to look at first parallel, and afterwards into the cockpits of the American fighter bombers.

They swooped down to release their bombs along the length of the train. Passengers who had finished boarding minutes before poured out onto the sidings. The six Thunderbolts climbed steeply above the rumble of the explosions, and looped back to strike again. Without ammunition for our weapons we watched helplessly as they came down for a second attack. The pilots roared past us and opened up with their machine guns on the townsfolk and passengers milling about beside the train.

A couple of days later we were ordered to attend the funeral for the nine victims. One was a soldier, another was a woman working in air force communications, the rest were civilians.

The front line had caught up to us. American forces took Münster on April 3. Soviet forces were now fighting inside Berlin.

Shortly afterwards, we moved north to the vicinity of Kassel. When we arrived there we were asked if we would like to have the *Henschel Konigstiger Panzer*, the King Tiger tank, and if so, we could pick them up at the factory in Kassel. There was just one impediment. We were told that we could have as many tanks as we wanted except that there would not be any gun sight optics or radios.

What good, we asked him, was a tank without optics? We could forgo the radio but not the optics. So we declined. The next day another supply officer came to see us and asked if we wanted armored half-tracks, the *Schutzenpanzerwagen* (*SPW*). Our company leader said, "Let's get as many *SPWs* as possible." He sarcastically appended, "At least we won't have to walk." He then asked, "Who has a driver's permit?" Although quite a few men stepped forward he was still short of drivers. Next, he called for anyone who could drive a vehicle, and I stepped forward. I was thinking to myself that the *SPW* was basically the same as the half-tracks we had used in Russia. Except that those that we were issued on the Eastern Front were not armored. Besides, all I had to do was to get it into gear and I had seen that done hundreds of times.

Our new vehicles were what we referred to as half-automatic. The first and second gears were for driving through difficult terrain and gears three through seven were for normal driving on the road. It all seemed very simple.

We were told to pick up our *SPWs* at a vehicle depot in a little village set high up in the hilly countryside about eight miles outside of Kassel. We arrived quickly enough but getting vehicles was a somewhat long affair because each driver had to sign for his car and then get it fueled. When one driver was finished another driver took his place. Afterwards, everyone was on their own to get back to the company.

In the meanwhile, the afternoon had passed and darkness was slowly rounding out the shadows. By the time I had gotten my armored car a quarter moon was rising in the dark spring sky. We had been in the area for only two days and no one had a map. The use of headlights was forbidden. As I left the village, I kept looking up at the sky to keep myself evenly spaced between the black shapes of the apple trees growing to either side of the roadway. Inside the driver's compartment I had an indicator that told me when I was steering to the left, right, or center. This feature was for the operator to use under fire, to ensure himself that he was driving in the desired direction.

I kept to the middle of the road with an eye on the tree tops and corrections to my turn indicator. I also kept a flashlight beside me because I didn't know the gearbox pattern and I needed it to see what gear I had pushed the shift into. Each time I looked towards the light and then looked up I was momentarily blinded and afterwards my surroundings seemed doubly dark.

To make matters worse, I wasn't sure how far I needed to drive. All I knew was that we would encounter someone who would signal us with a flashlight where we were to turn off into the assembly area.

Soon after leaving the village the narrow road began winding up a steep hillside. All of a sudden in the dark I saw lights waving me to the right. To my right there was only an embankment leading straight down to the valley floor. Confused, I inched my way over to the edge until I didn't dare go any farther, stopped, and set the hand brakes. Out of the darkness came the familiar growl of a huge King Tiger tank. Workers from the Kassel factory used the safety of darkness to transfer their tanks to the depot. The big tracks were as high as the sides of my car and we barely squeezed past one another.

I was driving uphill again, using the flashlight to down shift, when I realized that I couldn't go very fast. I was straining to see in the darkness ahead of me when smoke began filtering through the driver's visor slit carrying with it the smell of Bakelite. It was then I realized that I still had my hand brakes locked on. The brake drums on the inside of the wheels were red hot. I immediately reached down to release the brake lever and burnt my fingertips. It was late at night before I reported back to my company.

The next morning the order came to move out. Each *SPW* had seven guys assigned to it and to defend ourselves we had two machine guns mounted on top. I was gathering my men together just prior to leaving when I was told to exchange my half-track for another one. They were all new so I didn't mind, until I got in.

I stepped up into the driver's compartment and found that the gear box was of French manufacture. Called a Variarex gear box, it was completely different from the one that I had acquainted myself with the night before. I had no idea how to operate it. What was clear to me, was that the guy who had exchanged vehicles obviously had some influence with the company leader. I supposed that he was just as adept with cooked brakes.

Vehicle by vehicle the company departed our bivouac area and started uphill. I got mine going but it was going slow. I couldn't get the transmission out of first gear. We crept along like a snail until reaching the hilltop when I pushed in the clutch and began freewheeling to gain speed. On the next incline the three tons of steel quickly slowed to its previous painfully slow crawl. No matter what I tried I was unable to move through the proper sequence of gears. We had been the last one out of our assembly area and because we were moving so slow, I had lost sight of the truck in front of me. On the next downhill, I called to the guys with me and said hold on to everything.

As soon as I depressed the clutch it was like my *SPW* had hit ice. We shot down the serpentine. Our steel bucket vibrated noisily. The tires were humming. The tracks squealed in protest. The noise mounted to an unbearable pitch. The sideways glances and looks of disgust that had accompanied my struggle up the other side had been replaced by wide open mouths and eyes. The roller coaster ride worked. At the bottom I glimpsed one of our vehicles and saw which direction they were heading. Slowing to a crawl, I called for someone to look up front for a vehicle manual and find out how to operate the gear box. That was when we discovered that the Variarex had a knob that required turning prior to going into the different gears. The driver had to turn the transmission knob, press it down and depress the clutch, push the shift forward, pull it back, and let the clutch go. After I read that, there was nothing to it, and we quickly caught up with the rest of the company.

One constant problem was a lack of fuel. We were being given a poor grade of synthetic gasoline. To supplement our supplies we started paying close attention to the American Mustangs carrying auxiliary fuel tanks. At the end of a mission the pilots would release their surplus fuel pod. We watched carefully where these tanks fell because oftentimes we found more than 30 gallons of high octane gasoline inside. This was siphoned out and mixed with our own gasoline before dividing it between the squad's three armored half-tracks.

Our *SPWs* were equipped with two sets of wheels. The ones in the front drove the whole thing and then you had the wheels supporting the tracks. Among the rear wheels was one set outfitted with a special bolt. If the track became skewed or placed under too much tension the bolt sheared releasing the strain on the track and saving it from being broken. Each *SPW* came with a toolbox with between 6 and 12 extra bolts, and it was a very easy task to replace the bolt and retighten the track.

Because of the tracks you had to watch yourself while turning or going backwards because you could pick up a piece of wood in the forest and get it jammed between the wheels increasing the stress on the track and shearing the bolt. Everybody had that experience with the bolt on one occasion or another.

My turn came one night when I was sent out to pick up some of our men threatened with envelopment. They were under fire barely 100 yards in front of the Americans and so I came in driving fast. When I reached them I had to make a tight turn, the bolts broke and the tracks loosened. The only way to avoid further problems was to drive in reverse and so I did for nearly three miles through the dark. If the track had spilled off over the wheels we would have been in real trouble. The Americans were probing left and right and I wasn't about to stop and discover that someone else was already in the vicinity. As soon as we had gotten far enough into the rear I took the time to replace the bolt. To have stopped sooner simply would have jeopardized everyone I had been trying to rescue, including myself.

A couple of days later we camouflaged our two machine guns in the fields to the left and right of the road leading into a village about 500 yards away. Just after setting up I was driving the *SPW* into the village when I heard both machine guns firing. I drove back out and saw four American jeeps, each with a small trailer, sitting on the road leading past our position.

My machine gunners had let them pass and watched as the Americans stopped and brought out maps. Evidently they felt that a wrong turn had been made and were checking their maps against the name on the village sign. It was at that moment that they discovered they were indeed lost. When the last jeep began to maneuver around to drive away my squad fired its machine guns across the road. We had tracers in our ammo so they could see exactly how close we were shooting past them. All the Americans stopped what they were doing except the driver of the first jeep, who tried to escape by accelerating and drove right into the gun fire.

When I got to the scene the Americans were standing there with their hands raised. There were nine of them, ten including the dead driver. There was only one officer, a Captain Chamberlain. I have always remembered his name because of the pre-war British prime minister. When we checked them for weapons we discovered that each was carrying a .45 caliber side arm and knives of a sort that we had never seen before. We also checked all the wrist watches because we had a standing order to take away anything that was of military issue. We were not allowed to touch personal belongings such as non-military issue wrist watches or rings.

I loaded the prisoners into my armored car and drove them into the village where my company leader told me to take them back to our headquarters in the next town.

I was alone with nine prisoners standing in the back of my *SPW*. I was occupied with driving and completely unable to defend myself. I couldn't have gotten my pistol out if my life had depended on it. Fortunately for me they were not in the mood for a fight.

During the short drive I made a sign for a cigarette and said several times, "*Zigarette*" "*Zigarette*." One of the guys took a package out of his field jacket and handed it to me. I shook one out and returned the package. I remember the look of disbelief on his face. But I had no intention of taking the whole pack.

Everything had remained quiet during my absence. I didn't want to give away our ambush site, so upon returning I ordered some of my men to steer the jeeps as I towed them into the village out of view. Only when we had taken the jeeps and trailers into town did we bother to check what was inside. One of my companions understood a little English and was able to tell us that we had captured some regiment's Easter mail, including about a dozen cakes of some kind. We also discovered cartons and cartons of Camel and Lucky Strike cigarettes, German sparkling wine, and German hard liquor. The latter had been collected from private homes. Nazi party and Hitler Youth daggers were mixed in with their loot.

On the floor of one jeep I found an American field jacket and put it on. It was early April, it was still cold, and I didn't have a proper overcoat. Actually, in the driving compartment of the armored car it was such close quarters that an overcoat would have hindered my movements. Four large pockets were evenly spaced over the front and into these I stuffed cigarettes and chewing gum. We also found K-rations. These were something new to us. Here was every man's food from pork and beans and I believe something resembling ham and rice, to little tin cans only an inch high, with cheese inside. For us it was like Christmas.

We got the impression that many of the men were from the Northeast because there were newspapers from Boston and New York. The guy who could read some English showed us the obituaries of soldiers that gave a lot of details about their passing. This was quite unlike our obituaries that gave little more than a man's name and the general location of his death. We departed the village soon after. We left all of the mail on the jeeps and trailers and for the next couple of days we were really living good thanks to the Americans' rations.

From there on we did little fighting. Everyday the Americans came closer and closer, and every evening we had to retreat. During the day we were holding them and as soon as it was getting dark we exchanged our position for one farther back.

The Kassel region is mountainous. In the evenings sitting on a hilltop you could see over the whole countryside and the roads parallel to ours were full of American trucks.

With such a fluid front line the possibility of encirclement was becoming more and more likely. Sometimes during the day the Americans passed us for a mile or two. You had to be careful when retreating not to make them aware that you were still inside their new positions.

Our company leaders often talked about the *Wunderwaffe* that was still "somewhere" and how "someday" this wonder weapon would win the war. Nobody believed this, and whenever this sort of pep talk occurred everyone had a smirk on their face.

On Saturday, April 6, we were billeted by a farmer. The farm was situated in the rolling hillside close to a river and bridge. The owner was alone with his young daughter and he asked me, and I suppose others as well, to stay behind. He was afraid that on his own he couldn't protect his daughter from the Americans and proposed to hide the two of us in his barn. I refused and the next morning we said our good-byes.

As was my habit I took the rear guard and was, therefore the last to leave. When I finally got under way with my squad the other two armored cars had already passed over the crest of the next hill. I had just crossed over the bridge when the whole thing exploded showering us with pebble-sized debris. The bridge had been rigged for detonation and someone must have been hidden in plain sight and held off until we got over. At the same moment we cleared the bridge a platoon of Americans arrived at the farm and started shooting at us with their .50 caliber machine gun. Their response was too little, too late and in seconds we were out of range.

On the afternoon of Sunday, April 7, we were going backwards again and this time our fears came true. With the front line so flexible we had grown used to being very cautious. That evening our path took us along a road that paralleled the forest edge and then made a sharp turn. We stopped about a mile away from the curve and discovered that the Americans were already there. They had established an ambush site where the road made a sharp turn to the left into the forest. It was our only escape route so we decided that we would have to make a breakthrough. We three leaders of the half-track squads agreed that the best tactic called for all of us to go into the curve blazing away with our machine guns, at which time everyone would duck and try to get away. We were hoping that our suppressing fire coming in would give us the break we needed to escape.

We started off. I was the last *SPW* and now habit decided my fate. Just as I was gaining speed driving into that trap my engine started stuttering. The mixed gas was failing me just when I needed it most. When the engine began faltering my speed dropped and a gap grew between the first two cars and my own. I was slowing, the gap was widening, and I was unable to keep up with the rest of the squad. It quickly must have become obvious to the Americans manning the ambush site that here would be an easy target.

I watched when the first two cars reached the turn and everyone inside stopped firing, got down, and headed off around the curve. At that instant, all the fire concentrated on my armored car.

The machine gun and rifle bullets hitting the *SPW* sounded like you were sitting inside a metal barrel and a crowd was pelting it with stones. I had about two inches of glass in the slit opening in front of my eyes. With all the bullets hitting the armor I closed my armored outlook to protect the glass and all I had then was a very small slit of about half an inch. When I was between 10 and 15 yards from the turn I turned my steering wheel to the left. I hit the curve but the turn indicator was showing that I wasn't getting the car to respond. I reached down and pulled the lever beside my seat, hoping to brake the left-track and use the right-track to spin us around. The lever had no effect, and before I knew it we had left the road and hit a tree square on.

I was sitting there looking at the brown leather gloves on my hands thinking to myself that if I hold up my hands they might shoot at them. I pulled the gloves off. I also realized that I was wearing the American jacket so I wriggled out of that as well before I got out of my seat. When the three men behind me jumped out they were met by more firing from the Americans. I could hear that one of my friends was badly wounded.

I was hesitant to move, yet I was also afraid that the Americans would toss a grenade into the back. The driver's seat was very close quarters so after shedding that jacket, I wriggled around and found a washcloth, more gray than white, and put it up. From outside I heard, "Come Here!" "Come Here!"

My partner in the front seat beside me hadn't moved so I tapped him and told him to come on only to discover that he was already dead. The machine gun fire that had penetrated the armor killing my companion must have also damaged my steering hydraulics. I've often thought about it and that is the only explanation I can come up with, otherwise I would have made the turn.

We were standing there with our hands up and they came over and checked us for weapons. They patted us down and made me remove my pistol belt. Their quick search missed a palm-sized Walther in my hip pocket. My wounded friend was lying there. I don't know if he jumped out with his weapon or if the Americans thought that the first men out were attacking, or what. He was in extreme pain, lying there on the ground bleeding. I had offered first aid to countless men and without hesitating or reflecting I quickly moved to help. Just as I was kneeling down someone struck me hard from behind with his rifle butt. I tried to tell them what was obvious to me; he was seriously wounded under the rib cage and needed immediate attention. I wanted to get him bandaged. Apparently I made myself understood because one of the soldiers spoke into his walkie-talkie and soon after a corpsman arrived. That was the first time I saw a walkie-talkie and the last time I ever saw my friend.

In the meantime, they had begun searching the rest of my men. They discovered the American cheese and cigarettes in their pockets and each one in turn got knocked around with rifle butts. All the while they were talking to us. I'm sure they were asking where we had gotten these items, but of course we couldn't answer them.

I didn't have anything on me. I had stored everything in the pockets of the American jacket and that was still out of sight in the car.

We walked back to a nearby village through the cool, long shadows of the early evening. On the way someone made it understood that they wanted to drink and we stopped briefly at a stream. When no one was looking I pushed my Walther under the leaves lining the bank.

We were locked with other German soldiers in the garage of a private home. A short while later another armored car crew were captured at the same corner where my men and I had been taken prisoner. When they came to the garage the new prisoners began asking, "Who was in that first armored car that was ambushed?"

"Why?" I asked.

"Well," he answered, "the Americans are furious. They found one of their field jackets inside the car stuffed with their rations and cigarettes. They are insisting that we are plundering American prisoners for their gear and food."

Although that was not the case, the new arrivals had taken a beating for it and so they were pretty mad. I kept my mouth shut and nothing more came of it.

We were locked inside overnight. The following day we were transported west to the next village where I experienced my first disappointment about American soldiers.

CHAPTER VII

1946
Bits and Pieces

GERMAN army regulations specified that you took away from your prisoners everything that was of military issue, whether compasses, watches, or weapons but never personal possessions. I always adhered to this rule and never questioned that others did likewise.

When we arrived at the village we were made to stand in line and the soldiers there informed us that they were going to take all our medals away. We were instructed to remove our awards from our jackets and hand them over.

Because I had received the Iron Cross second class it was represented by a ribbon sewn below my collar, but I took whatever else I was wearing off my jacket and dropped it into the dirt in front of me. This one American who came up to me was furious and yelling, but I refused to bend over and pick up anything to hand to him. I couldn't understand what was being said, except for one word that came out clearly and repeatedly: Fuck-Fuck-Fuck. At first I was unaware of the meaning. But it was a word I learned very fast from our captors.

The Americans we encountered were interested in everything. I had my engagement ring, fountain pen, and wristwatch, a gift from my uncle, robbed from me and I was angry about it. I saw soldiers with four and more wristwatches, and fountain pens by the dozens. For myself this was a shock. In my experience with military discipline this sort of thing was unheard of. I will not say that all the German soldiers I knew were angels. But here it was not being done by one or two but by a whole company and in the presence of their officers.

Next they took our mess kits away from us. When they examined mine they broke the handle of my spoon in half and threw it on the ground, probably in response to my obstinacy. My knife, fork, and the remainder of my kit were tossed onto a big heap. When they were not looking I snatched up the bowl half of my spoon so I wouldn't have to eat with my fingers.

On my third day of captivity we were moved to a larger prison camp. This was a prisoner collection center and transit compound. Prisoners were being brought in from everywhere and dropped off to stay for a night or two.

When you are a prisoner the first thing on your mind is when do we get something to eat. That evening in the transit camp we were forced to divide a small can of pork and beans between two guys. There wasn't much. Each of us got maybe three to four spoonfuls and that was it. Feeding ourselves was made even more difficult because most men were missing a knife, fork, spoon or plate. I picked up a tin can for use as a bowl and shared it with another guy.

I didn't know it then but it would be weeks before we could wash ourselves—we had no extra water. The only available water was for drinking. It took a whole day of standing in line to get drinking water, and then you were only given a cup or two.

There was a field filled with supplies beside the camp. Convoys of two-and-a-half ton trucks were coming daily to this depot. I noticed that instead of departing empty the trucks were being loaded with prisoners.

I was standing around the main gate trying to take in as much as I could, when the German interpreter entered and announced he needed thirty men. I volunteered right away. We marched over to the field and set about unloading C-ration boxes off the arriving trucks. Naturally, when you handle a box in the right way, and hit it the right way, it will split open and spill its contents. By such means, I got a little more to eat on this occasion. When I had the opportunity I snatched one of the tin cans from a broken box and hid it by putting it all the way down my pant leg. When we returned to the camp gate we were made to stand with our arms up while we were searched. Other guys who had done the same thing as me, had hidden their cans in their jackets. The Americans were getting angry about it although everything they found they just tossed into the dirt. The guy who searched me went up to my chest and down to my knees. My one can was safe and I felt I could last another day. The following morning we were transported back to the Rhine River on trucks that had brought more supplies to the depot.

Everyone climbing aboard was made to stand facing the front. When I thought that the truck was loaded the driver rolled forward two to three yards and hit the brakes, slamming and squeezing everyone forward. The Americans who were standing at the tailgate began hitting the guys farthest in the back with sticks and in this way made room for 10 or 15 more of us before they closed up the rear.

Many of the drivers were black and they were driving as if there was a race on, scaring the hell out of everyone. We had nothing to hold onto except the men to your left and right. When the driver turned into a curve the mass of us shifted in the opposite direction. Our journey took us along the Lahn River valley road where there were plenty of curves.

Some drivers had something similar to modern tractor trailers with flexible sidewalls. These were loaded in the same manner as what I had experienced, but the thin sides posed an additional danger. When the driver was going into a sharp curve the weight of the prisoners pushing to the outside broke the frail sidewalls, and some trailers overturned. There were quite a few unnecessary deaths and numerous injuries.

Our destination was Andernach, a prisoner of war camp on the Rhine near Koblenz. Everyone was interrogated there. My interrogator spoke perfect German. He knew what units I had belonged to, where my units had been stationed and had fought. They knew exactly what I had been doing since my last unit was organized right up to my capture. After my interrogation I was sent into a different part of the camp.

In Andernach we shared the contents of one carton of C-rations among twenty-five guys. Each one of us had to find his own empty tin can to eat from, and the Americans left lots of these lying around. Upon opening a carton we always found plenty of little boxes and plenty of little cans. Typically, after receiving their food a group could be found with two guys sitting on a blanket and twenty-three guys standing around in a circle watching like hawks what the two were doing. Everything was opened and twenty-five portions were made.

Whatever was in the C-ration containers was divided into 25ths. Each man got five beans, maybe two and a half crackers and a piece of cheese. When we were done dividing everything, I could hold my ration for that day in one hand. A lot of men traded away anything that they had been able to hold onto for more food. Gold wedding rings were a common item of exchange traded to camp cooks for bread. These cooks were also German prisoners but they were not there to prepare us food. The Americans kept German prisoners in the kitchen for the permanent German staff working at Andernach. Only the camp staff was allowed warm meals, those of us in transit were given cold food. Although I found things tough, I discovered later that life was much more unpleasant in the camp at Kreuznach, south of Mainz.

After several days in the camp the rumor was that we were being shipped to the U.S.A. One evening the guards came into the camp and said everyone who is wounded should go to the main gate. I was wounded in December and this was late April, nonetheless I decided to say that I was still wounded and limped out to the gate, my right arm bent inside my jacket. When I got to the main gate the interpreter stated in a questioning voice, "You are wounded?" And I replied, "Yes, through my arm and leg," and I said, "I have problems walking." I was told to get in line and we marched to the railroad where we were loaded standing up in open-topped rail cars. We had no water and nothing to eat. Not having water was difficult. Each time the steam engine stopped to take on water, we were hoping that we would be allowed a drink. Nothing was ever given to us. Any of the prisoners who jumped down and walked up front to get water were immediately fired on by the guards. But some continued to do it.

After we crossed into Belgium our transport seemed to lose its urgency and sometimes we were shunted off onto side tracks and made to wait. I had gotten myself included among men wounded much more recently than I had in hopes of getting better living conditions. But the category "wounded" now mattered little.

When the Belgians noticed that there was a prisoner transport many went onto railroad overpasses to throw stones. Because we were packed so tightly together, man against man, we had no chance to defend ourselves. We couldn't even bend to avoid the missiles. We had quite a few injuries in my car and deaths in others, before the Americans put a guard sitting astride the sideboards with his rifle at ready. When we approached an overpass the guards would fire a couple of rounds into the air to warn off the rock throwers. That was enough to give us some protection.

Our nonstop journey continued to Liege, my mother's hometown. When we had stopped, we were marched to the site of a big factory where other prisoners told us we would be fed that evening. We had waited days to eat and were famished. Just as before, we were told to find ourselves tin cans to eat from. I found a nice one-gallon can that was clean with no sharp edges, and of course I still had my little spoon. When evening came we were ordered into line and told that now we would be fed.

We shuffled single file through large sliding doors into a big hall-like building. The lighting was so poor inside that it tended to emphasize the gloominess of the spacious interior. When I passed the door somebody hidden in the dark threw a piece of bread at me. I couldn't believe that it was almost a quarter of a loaf! I was able to catch it and since I had my can in my hand I shoved the bread inside my jacket out of sight.

I then saw that we were going to get a hot cooked cereal. There was a guy with a large ladle standing behind a big pot of this mixture. He would dig in and just move the ladle towards you as he turned his wrist. If you were not ready your portion was on the floor and you were made to move on. No one was allowed to wait for another swing of his arm. Luckily, I caught his swing right in my can. That was all we were getting, but for us that was already plenty.

After my eyes had adjusted to the gloom I noticed that there were rows and rows of high tables for standing and eating. We were still walking. I assumed that they were directing the first man in line towards the exit and that everyone would follow through until all the tables were occupied and then we would be allowed to start eating. Because the grain was so hot, I picked at mine with my spoon, waiting to enjoy it when the line stopped.

I was slowly sliding one foot and then the other forward while swallowing small spoonfuls, when suddenly all of the tables were behind me and I was at the exit. I was met there by a guard who motioned me to toss my can to one side and throw the bread to the other.

My bread was hidden, so I tossed my tin of cereal. I glanced around and saw the others trying to snatch bites from their bread. Nearly everyone lost their cereal and bread; forced to throw it away on a garbage pile.

What a surprise! I was stunned and all that came to mind was the parable of Jesus when he fed the people in the desert. We had been given food and had the food taken away from us. And worst of all, it was thrown into the waste.

That night we were locked inside another large empty building where we slept on the concrete floor. The following morning we marched back to the railway station and during the next leg of our journey the train crossed the border into France, to the village of Attichy and a prison camp of the same name. It was the first week of May.

From Attichy's railroad station we walked about three miles to a high plateau overlooking the Aisne River. My first impression was that this site must have been an airfield during the war. Here the Americans had built a tremendously large camp, subdivided into numerous interior units. A main road ran through the middle of the camp off of which were side roads leading into the smaller compounds. Each of the subdivisions held about 2,000 to 3,000 prisoners and there may have been 20,000 to 30,000 prisoners in the whole camp. All of us slept in tents.

We discovered that now we would get regular feedings. In Attichy, our breakfast came at noon, our lunch in the evening and supper at midnight. The midnight feeding was always some kind of cereal. One person in my tent group decided to save his cereal for the "morning" feeding. He left it in his can and put it at the head of his sleeping position. Someone passing by during the night discovered the bulging contour of the can pressing against the tent cloth. Its significance given away, he lifted the tent side and stole the container.

Later a couple of men were caught stealing food and they were given such a beating that they nearly died. They were lucky that they were not thrown in the latrine. All of us were hungry—near starving—and stealing from one another was the lowest thing anyone could have done.

During our first week there we were issued one packet of tobacco and cigarette papers. I got the tobacco issue one time. It stopped immediately after peace was officially declared on May 10.

I was surprised in this camp, as well as the others I had been in, to encounter postal and railroad employees. These men were not in any way involved with the military but because of their "ranks" and uniforms the Americans had rounded them up with regular combatants.

As at Andernach, I discovered that it was helpful to be around the main gate because it was easier to gather information there. Sometimes what you heard was just rumor, sometimes it was true. Either way it gave you something to think about and perhaps even the opportunity to act on it, in your favor.

Early one morning the guards came looking for prisoners who were able to work. Once again I volunteered and I was sent to another camp near Laon. This camp was smaller than Attichy and contained approximately 2,500 prisoners working in an American supply depot.

I stayed several months at Laon. It was divided into a grid, much like the camp at Attichy. Each smaller group or company consisted of six tents, each with its own kitchen, the whole bordered by roads. I slept with twenty-three other men in a tent designed for twelve. We were sleeping on straw and each one of us had a blanket. On the one hand it was extremely close quarters, on the other hand this kept us warm. For the first time we also had toilet facilities with showers.

The Americans had huge Nissan huts that were used as warehouses and they kept one company of their soldiers inside the depot for administrative purposes. In that depot you had everything an army needed from nails to coffins. Two shifts of prisoners worked around the clock unloading the railroad cars that were arriving daily from the coast.

Our day began after breakfast when we were marched out to the railroad. We generally worked about 50 minutes before the guards would declare a cigarette break. We didn't have cigarettes and the soldiers were not allowed to give us any. There were quite a few guards with big hearts who would light a cigarette, make you a signal, walk behind some crates and emerge from the other side. If you followed you would find the cigarette there on a crate.

Others would light a cigarette and drop it on the ground. Those close by would move towards it and the guard would take one step forward and grind away with his boot until there was nothing left. I never let myself go so far as to retrieve anything, neither food nor cigarettes, off the ground.

Once I volunteered for night shift. I was issued a small forklift with solid rubber tires. I had never driven a forklift before, but I moved around it, checking the fuel, oil, and water as if I knew what I was doing. While checking the radiator I noticed that it was low on water, so I started it up and drove over to a hose. Driving seemed to be easy enough after you got used to the rear wheels turning rather than the front. I turned on the water hose and I was filling and filling the reservoir but there wasn't much pressure and the water just seemed to be trickling in. I didn't know that when it was full a tube channeled the overflow onto the ground. I was standing there waiting for the water to overflow the top, not realizing that the water had for some time been running through the tube and away from the lift across the ground where I couldn't see it. A young 2d Lieutenant came up and started yelling, but I didn't pay him much attention. He bent over, pointing with his finger while repeatedly yelling Water! When I realized why he was so excited I made my best Charlie Chaplin face, replaced the cap and calmly drove away. It was easy to play dumb. I didn't understand English.

The guards carried flashlights but there were enough dark corners that we could do our work with plenty of time for mischief.

On another night shift, while busy unloading a freight train, we discovered one boxcar full of dozens and dozens of grayish-colored lightweight metal bars. We didn't know what they were for, but with so many men together from so many backgrounds we soon found out that it was natrium, a mineral that burns when placed in water.

After learning this we had to try some. We broke one of the bricks over a railroad track and collected the chunks. We found an old can and because we didn't have any water we all took turns urinating in it. Afterwards we went around the corner and one of us stretched his arm out and dropped a small piece into the urine. One to two seconds later the piece shot into the air with a CLOOP! noise. We quickly discovered that you could use it several times, and each time the piece reduced in size.

The following evening we found a pipe and buried one end of the tube in the ground. We filled the pipe with water and dropped a small chunk of the natrium into it. The hollow, WHUSH-like sound was just like a grenade launcher. After further discussion and experimentation we agreed on how to best use our discovery.

There was a latrine inside the depot. The facility consisted of a large tent covering an eight-seat trench toilet. There were guys in our detail who didn't like working and they were always sneaking off to the latrine where they sat with their pants around their ankles. To the guards passing by they looked like they were doing their business. The problem was, however, when they were absent we were short handed and these guys could disappear for up to half an hour while the rest of us did their work.

After the discovery of the natrium we found that if we went to the toilets and pretended to be sitting there we had the opportunity to drop a piece in the hole on the way out. Seconds after walking away there was a BOOM! and the piece flew out, hit the underside of the tent and went back in, erupting from the latrine three or four more times in quick succession. The BOOM! BOOM! BOOM! sent frightened combat conditioned soldiers leaping from their seats twisting and stumbling from the tent with their pants around their ankles.

We stole from the American kitchen. The American company stationed inside the depot had its own kitchen and mess hall and they were very finicky about the garbage. Three cans were always located outside their mess tent. When the guys were finished eating they tossed leftover coffee in one can, bread in another and whatever remained in a third. These cans were scrubbed clean everyday.

We would sneak around their mess tent and try to snatch bread from the bread can. When the sergeant major caught a fellow he would be made to sit down inside the kitchen and forced to eat from a three pound can of sliced bacon until he threw up. That was not the end of it. For the next two or three days after being force-fed, that person suffered from terrible diarrhea that led to dehydration.

Another favorite punishment of his was to make men stand in the sun without their shirts, balancing a two yard-long wooden beam, the dimensions of a railroad tie, on their shoulders until they collapsed. Other times the sergeant major confined anyone caught stealing food from the trash in a small wire cage beside the front gate. Before they were locked in he would shave their eyebrows and eyelids. The shaving was painful enough, but when the hairs started growing in again, it was even worse. The blunt sharp ends of the new growth on the lower lids poked and cut the inside of the upper lid, irritating and inflaming the skin until they were swollen shut. It was impossible to keep your eyes open and too painful to close them. The result was horrible to endure. These tortures continued until the Red Cross made a surprise visit that resulted in his transfer.

Some mess sergeants poured gasoline on top of the garbage so no one could pick anything out. Still others would let us know that the can with the bread would be placed around the corner so that we could approach unseen. Every little bit helped.

The Americans regularly used a detail of three to four men to bring water from the main gate to be used for cooking, drinking, and cleaning. That was a big deal for us, because extra food was allotted that group. When I had the luck to be chosen I was really excited about having more to eat. We were unaware that our bodies had become unaccustomed to even near normal portions of food and the result was painful diarrhea. Because of the diarrhea you didn't gain anything, you lost. For a couple of days afterwards I felt miserable, and was so weak I was unable to move.

Before working in the morning, we ate a small portion of cereal with one or two biscuits. At lunchtime we marched back to the camp where we were normally fed soup and bread. After one hour we marched out again to the work site and remained there until late in the afternoon. The food we were being given was not enough to fill you and I believe there may have been a reason we were always kept hungry. As long as you were hungry you never talked about women. They could have sent a hundred naked women through that camp and no one would have paid them the least bit of attention. How much bread will I have tonight would have been a more appropriate thought. All we had on our minds was food. We were given a little too much food to die but not enough to live normally.

The camp bread was cooked in small loaves, about 10 x 10 inches square. The middle of these loaves were thicker than the ends. Each day our cooks were trying to divide the bread evenly, sometimes into twelve, sometimes into sixteen slices. When it was time to eat we had to line up in front of our mess area and there was always some shuffling around to get the largest piece.

We had one fellow with us who was a banker and somehow that guy always figured out how to get the thickest slice of bread.

Some of the smart ones would slip in front or behind him, but they were often getting smaller slices and were therefore, only cheating themselves.

From our camp we had a nice view of Laon and the gothic towers of its church. Prisoners heated nails and burned the scene into leather scraps and small pieces of wood that were traded to our guards for food.

We had a fantastic eighteen-man dance band with instruments provided by the Red Cross. Our band played for the Americans who generally staged a dance in the depot once a month to which they invited the local French girls. During these dances the German prisoners provided all the table service.

We also formed a theater in this camp. When you get 2,000 plus people together there is often lots of talent, from musicians and film industry personnel, to professionals from the opera. We equipped our actors by extending the camp barter system to the French civilians.

We were hungry but the French were too. We had a group of guys who were responsible for hauling camp garbage to a municipal dump. The French locals were always there, scouring the refuse for food. The German prisoners exchanged the camp garbage for something they could use. It was in this way that the theater group secured women's underclothes, stockings, and shoes.

We attended our own theater once a week. On opening nights all the American officers and soldiers, who always sat in the first couple of rows, were in attendance. One of our stage plays had numerous women's roles and when the curtain went up the guys playing the female parts were so natural that you would have sworn you were watching a real woman. It must have had the same effect on the American officers because one of them stood up, called for the guards, and closed the curtains. The military police made sure that there were no women on stage before the play was allowed to resume. Naturally this drew a big laugh.

Our cooks made up our soccer team. Only they could play because they were the only ones with nearly full stomachs. The rest of us were in no condition to run nonstop over a soccer field. We would have collapsed.

Every little bit you were getting was a highlight, and the theater and dance helped us to forget our personal miseries. I am not fatalistic. But I couldn't help thinking about how I had escaped Russian snipers and mines, how Ludwig had taken my place at the window, how I was allowed to exchange leave with another man just before the Russian offensive that wiped out the 195th, how I had been wounded when my next unit was lost in the Battle of the

Bulge. How many incidents? How many times? There had been too many to remember and others that were too hard to forget. I always accepted the position of rear guard and so my squad and I were captured. If I had been the first or even the second car the others would not have escaped. After seeing a stage play or hearing the band my outlook was always a little more optimistic. Perhaps I was even a little more determined to survive and to remember others.

In Laon we received goods from Cherbourg that were in turn, processed and shipped to Germany. There were frequent attempts to break out using the materials passing through our camp. For example, the Americans were shipping boxcars full of camouflage netting that filled the containers up to the ceiling. Some of us hid in it but the guard dogs signalled that we were there.

Big wooden boxes used to ship large, oversized metal parts were also common. The boxes were nearly a yard wide, two yards high and sometimes nearly twice as long. These were always arriving on the train cars and we stored the empty ones inside the depot. Some men took secret possession of them and used the containers to store provisions. Cans were filled with water, dry bread was stockpiled, and sleeping material was hidden away. Whenever this was the case, other prisoners were politely steered away from the crates.

As the time passed, I believe we prisoners took on less of an importance to our captors. The security slowly relaxed, and more and more internal camp duties were performed by captives with a greater and greater measure of freedom. After a while, the whole camp was being run with minimal American participation. German prisoners received the goods, sat in the main office and processed the invoices and loading papers. It was during this time that we stenciled the big boxes with addresses in Germany. Our friends got inside, the things were nailed shut and loaded on a flat car. Because it was sitting out in the open, it escaped scrutiny. As far as I am aware these men made it back to Germany.

Bread commissioned from local bakers was delivered to the cooks in big, triple-layered paper sacks. Towards winter I went to the kitchen and bartered with the cooks so I could take one of the sacks with me. At night I was slipping into that paper sack, drawing it up to my hips. Then I was able to double my blanket over my shoulders. Although it always made a lot of noise when I was getting in and out, it helped me to stay warm during the night.

I volunteered to work as a driver and was transferred to another camp closer to Compiègne. We were about 40 to 50 prisoners attached to an American battalion living in a chateau, three to four miles from our camp. This time our camp consisted of regular barracks. We were told that during the war a German air force communications company had been housed there.

Polish guards were stationed on the outside of the camp fence. They were not allowed inside our compound. The Poles patrolled both the supply depot and the prison camp. These were all Polish, civilian volunteer units, with Polish officers. All of the Poles wore blue helmets and dark blue uniforms.

For my first couple of weeks there I went to the chateau and worked in the American mess hall, or in the yard cutting wood. I also worked in the stable attending to the horses. That was where I saw my first American woman in uniform. They would come out to the chateau to ride and we had to saddle and hold the horses when they mounted. The women were always very nice and often gave us a package of cigarettes.

When another call for drivers was made, I again volunteered. They picked twelve of us, put us in a truck, and drove us southwest to Reims where a large German airfield had been transformed into a motor pool. The enclosure was filled with vehicles from the gate to the horizon. Any type of transportation you might need was there, from the big rigs with trailers to jeeps. We all received what were referred to as 6x6s, with three axles.

I had never driven that type of shift before and due to my past experiences, I was determined not to start in first gear. Pretty soon I discovered that it was a simple H-pattern with a fifth gear for the open road. I pushed the shift immediately into second gear and after depressing the clutch I started the engine. I held the clutch in until I was told to go. In the dark I made it to the outskirts of Laon.

Laon is a medieval hillside town with lots of streets going up and down on the road to Compiègne. Heading uphill the motor started stuttering and I lost power. I pressed the clutch, braked, and started from second again. I was holding up the column but as long as I was going uphill I couldn't seem to change gear.

I went very slowly up to the crest of each hill until I angrily depressed the clutch, grabbed the gear shift knob firmly in my hand and pushed. The resulting racket from underneath the cab was horrendous. A loud grinding of metal on metal indicated that the gears weren't meshing smoothly and quietly. Instead each metal tooth, of each unyielding hardened steel gear, was hitting and deflecting the teeth of the gear revolving closest to it. It sounded as though I was implementing the self-destruction of the transmission. I continued to push until I had succeeded in forcing the transmission from second to third gear. Afterwards I glanced anxiously in my mirror several times, certain that I would be able to identify pieces of metal scattered on the blacktop behind me.

The next morning I was called to the main office and ordered to go with two other drivers to the depot at Laon. The first truck had a German driver and an American guard, the second and third trucks only had German drivers and because I was the last truck I had another American sitting beside me. It looked as though I would have a witness to the mechanical culprit I had mastered the evening before.

When it came time to change from second to third gear, I depressed the clutch and the same sound of metal striking metal filled the cab until the transmission gave way to the force I was exerting on the resistant gear shift. I gave a satisfied glance to my right just as my guard's look of shock was replaced by his yelling NO! NO! NO!, followed by a stream of words and hand gestures that I understood to mean stop, because we are changing places—NOW! He slid over behind the wheel and I climbed in the passenger side.

He explained by using simple words. "Clutch—two—times." And he showed me how he used the clutch pedal to disengage the gear, lifted his foot and went down again with the clutch before engaging the next gear. Everything went as smooth as silk. I didn't want to appear like a dummy so I yelled back, "German," and held up one finger. He just shook his head and drove on. I secretly watched him like a hawk whenever he was shifting gears. When it came my turn to drive everything worked like a charm.

We stayed at Laon for two days. I slept in my old camp and reacquainted myself with my buddies who hadn't been transferred out. While I was absent from Compiègne, all the drivers from our barracks took a driver's test. We had some professional drivers in our group possessing extensive experience and when I returned I discovered that some hadn't passed the test.

The morning after our return, I was called into the main office. A young Corporal Ralph Roth told me to get my truck out of its parking space and when I came back he climbed up beside me.

Our office building was right beside a small country road and you had to watch carefully for civilians. I approached the gate, looked to my right and left and he motioned me to my right. I left the compound and accelerated to 30 miles per hour. After a few miles he motioned me off the highway onto a dirt road. I downshifted, looked in my mirrors and used hand signals to turn left. I drove out about 100 feet and he indicated I should stop and return to camp. When he had made me stop I immediately assumed I had failed. I backed out using the most elaborate precautions possible even involving him, using sign language, to check on his right side for oncoming traffic.

I pulled up in front of the office to let him out and as he stepped down he turned and slowly said, "You-are-a-good-driver." I understood that much but I couldn't believe my luck and went to find the others.

I explained what I had done and asked how they could have failed. They replied that they thought that they were to go like hell. When we were transported, we had been chauffeured like the devil himself was driving and they had assumed that it was necessary to do the same. They had barely left the camp gate and they were accelerating faster and faster as they moved through the gears. When told to turn left they were moving too fast to downshift and they had to brake so hard they almost tossed the corporal through the windshield, and he didn't like that. The next day I had my driver's license signed by Corporal Roth and I still have it today.

I was assigned to the garbage detail and for a while I brought our garbage, and that of the Americans, to a nearby dump. I was shocked when I entered that garbage dump for the first time. The French were free of the Germans and they were American allies, and there they were waiting for our trucks so that they could go through the garbage just to find something to eat. The established exchange rate was one bottle of alcohol per one truck load of garbage. When we were captured and placed on such a small ration I didn't blame the Americans directly. When you have captured such a mass of men and you have to feed them your first priority remains the well being of your own troops. Prisoners are second and fed from whatever surplus you have. No army will put its own troops in jeopardy just to make sure that their prisoners had full stomachs. I guess I was surprised to find civilians in the same position.

Our camp commander was a 1st lieutenant of Polish descent but he didn't want anything to do with the Poles guarding the camp perimeter. We did him a number of favors.

He would often go into town and get drunk. On one occasion the locals stole the wheels from his jeep. Another time they stole everything except the shell of the jeep. When he came back, he went directly to our German camp leader named Schwartz, nicknamed "Blacky" by the Americans. The lieutenant was fearful to report how everything had been stolen. He revealed his dilemma to Blacky insisting that he needed a solution fast.

Every military vehicle had a long registration number stenciled on its hood. This number always corresponded with the vehicle's inventory paperwork. First, Blacky prepared the necessary paperwork in military triplicate. Afterwards we set off for the large motor pool at Reims where we had picked up our vehicles. When we departed the camp we had two triplicates. One was for our truck with the hood of the lieutenant's jeep hidden in the back. The other triplicate was for the jeep that had been stripped.

As with our camp, the office at Reims was being run by German prisoners. All the Americans were doing was providing half-ass guard services.

We went into the motor pool, chose a good looking jeep, unbolted its hood, and bolted on the hood of the lieutenant's jeep with the appropriate inventory number. Upon departing, we presented the triplicate for its release. The lieutenant was ecstatic and afterwards he did a lot of things for our group.

One day we heard unofficially that the camp was to be dismantled. When we caught wind of the rumor that we would be transferred it was the old question of—to where and when?

When word circulated of our transfer we were hoping that we would go to America and fearful that we would be given to the French. German prisoners who had been transferred from English to French authority had all of their belongings taken away. In contrast, the German prisoners from America often returned with two duffel bags filled with clothing and cigarettes. In the U.S. they were being paid 80 cents a day and they were allowed to buy whatever they needed at a camp store. Everyday I worked I also received 80 cents, on paper. My pay was held until I was released. The lieutenant promised us that if he discovered that they were going to transfer us to French control, he would falsify the necessary paperwork for us to go to Germany with the trucks. The arrangement was that after two days he would report the trucks as missing. Luckily for us, we drivers were ordered to go to Germany with our trucks, while the other camp members traveled by railroad car.

Near our camp there were about twelve German prisoners of war working for local farmers. These men were free to do as they liked on Sundays except that they didn't have anywhere to go. When they discovered that we were at the chateau they gained permission to enter our camp. When we first met them their German uniforms were in tatters so we outfitted them with surplus American uniforms. Every Sunday afternoon we gathered together and our camp cooks made cakes that we served with jam and chocolate. The cooks were issued exactly what was necessary to provide a certain number of meals for a certain number of men. If a surprise visit of the American's military police revealed surplus stock, it was automatically confiscated. The cooking for our visitors was from supplies that were secretly set aside from the main issue.

On our last Sunday in France we told them that we had our orders to leave for Germany. It was hard to look at their faces. They wanted to go along and for us that was no problem. The problem was that they were supposed to report back to their farms on Sunday evening and we were leaving on Tuesday. There was a two day period during which they would be expected at their farms. We needed to hide them.

In our camp there was a water tank over a story and a half high set on 8' x 8' stilts. The wooden, open-topped reservoir was covered by an enormous tarp that hung down the sides to the tops of the stilts. The olive drab canvas completely hid the platform the tank rested on. We told them the only place they could hide was to get around the water tank and stand there for two days.

On Monday morning French gendarmes and American military police searched every room, breaking open our ceilings and floors but they were unable to find anyone and left. The next morning at 10:00 A.M. our convoy was ready to go. The twelve came down the tower, hid in our trucks, and we drove off.

On the way from Compiègne to Germany we went via Metz to Homburg am Saar. Metz was our first overnight stay, and the first place we gassed up.

The Metz gas station was huge. Special hoses 20 feet long allowed everyone to gas up simultaneously. Once again, the whole operation was being run by German prisoners.

We were all dressed in American uniforms. We drivers always had one working uniform and one better one. We always saved the best one to make trips to town.

In the morning we would go to the motor pool, get our trucks and stop by the office and pick up our trip tickets. We had prisoners of war (POWs) on our backs and POWs on our front pant leg. Because we had our good uniforms on we simply marked ourselves with toothpaste and we were passed by the guard. Once the toothpaste had dried and we had brushed the powder off, we looked just like Americans.

We had mastered all of the American bad habits as well. We chewed big wads of gum so that our jaws were always in motion. When we were driving we stuck our left foot out the window and rested it on the mirror. The French always thought we were American and would ask for cigarettes which, when we had enough, we always shared. Unfortunately, we seldom had enough.

When we came into Metz the Germans working at the gas depot thought that we were Americans. Then they heard us talking. "Hey," they said, "Are you German?" "Where are you going?" "To Germany," we replied smugly.

When they asked, "Can you take us along?" I replied, "I can't say no or yes. I can say that what I don't see I don't know." We had stored all the beds from our barracks in the back of my 6x6 and behind that I towed a little trailer stockpiled with material from the motor pool. We were pretty well loaded. When I left I had two men from the Metz station secreted in the little trailer. All of the other drivers also had stowaways.

An American officer was leading the convoy in a jeep and beside him there were a couple of other men. A Polish guard was watching our last truck. Before leaving the lieutenant had instructed the Pole not to watch us, but rather, to watch that the French didn't steal something. So we were pretty free and the Pole was unaware of our new passengers.

We were leaving France. The bright green of early summer decorated the northern French countryside and the market squares of the numerous small towns dotting our route. Twin rows of plane trees, growing straight from grassy roadside banks, stood silent sentinel over our column's passage. We swung wide around the occasional bicycle rider.

It was in a distant field that a lone figure caught my attention. He was walking slowly behind a team of draft horses and he looked up as we neared. I quickly realized why he had attracted my gaze. He was wearing what once had been a black panzer uniform that now hung in tatters over his thin frame. Obviously, he was working for a local farmer.

When he saw our convoy, the first two fingers of his right hand moved to his lips, signalling that he wanted a cigarette. When I called to him in German he looked back in disbelief and stammered, "*Aber, du bist Deutscher*?!" I had hardly replied when he asked, "What are you doing dressed like Americans? Where are you going?" "To Germany," I said matter of factly.

"Can I come along?" he asked.

"Sure. Why not."

He ran to the team, laid the traces over the plow handles, ran back to my truck and jumped into the rear. He had forgotten all about the cigarette.

For German laborers to escape from a farm was easy. The problem was in crossing the Rhine River where the bridges had been destroyed. The only way to cross was on the military bridges and they were alternating one-way traffic.

Descending to the Rhine River we passed through a small village with even smaller streets and lots of tight curves. We came around one corner and were surprised by a guy who came right up to us and asked if we were German. He next asked if we were crossing the river. "I have been hiding here for five days and I cannot cross nor hide here anymore." We allowed him to get in the back of the truck in front of me.

At the bridge, every vehicle and driver were being checked. When we crossed they looked at our papers without paying too close attention to our trailers or trucks. As soon as we were over the Rhine we and our passengers were free of further scrutiny.

The next stop we made was on the Autobahn. The fellow we picked up just prior to crossing got off, and one by one so did several others along the way.

Whenever a driver had to drop someone he motioned to the one behind to slow down in order to shield the escape from the view of the Pole sitting with the driver of the last truck. A face would appear, a hand would wave and a prisoner would disappear into a roadside ditch.

That night when we came into Homburg we still had plenty of stowaways. The American lieutenant in charge ordered everyone into two lines and using his flashlight he started counting. When we left Compiègne we were about eighteen men and soon the lieutenant was counting 26, 27, 28. Then he yelled to the interpreter, "Tell these sons-of-bitches to stand in a line not in a circle!" Our interpreter explained the problem and he said that he was amenable to that, but only eighteen of us could go into the mess hall at one time. Afterwards, if there was any food remaining the others would be let in. The food was plentiful and everyone got to eat.

The following day we drove to Hanau near Frankfurt where the Americans were occupying a big German army base right on the Main River. We were still prisoners of war and although we had to sleep in tents again, thanks to our forethought, we at least had our bunks from the old barracks.

Six days a week, my job was to transport materials to nearby cities. Sometimes I was accompanied by an American, but more often than not I was alone. On Sundays the German population from the little village came around and we were able to ask that they send letters to our parents and let them know that we were all right. They did this for us, and even paid for our stamps.

In late May 1946, word came that we would be released. Farmers and coal miners were sent home immediately. The rest of us had to sign up for one year of work as a civilian while we continued to live in our camp. After one year we would be allowed to go home for good. In the meantime, we were told that we would be given furloughs so we could visit our families. At Hanau about 80 percent of the men signed up. Those who didn't were sent to prisoner of war camps in England, where some men remained for another year and a half.

When our new civilian status was official I received my furlough and visited my mother. I rode the train home and every time we passed into a different allied zone soldiers boarded and checked everyone's papers. It was just like traveling from one country to another. Fortunately, all of the goods I had been storing away escaped notice. I presented her with a duffel bag containing, among other things, real coffee secreted in a bottle, flour, and plenty of cigarettes. She didn't keep anything for herself. Instead, she carefully used small amounts of these items to barter for butter and milk, oil and potatoes. It was then that I discovered that the old farmer's son had been killed and apparently Juhle as well. I also found out how my father had survived.

At the very end of the war he was still fighting on the Russian front. There was a wounded German in no man's land between his position and that of the Russians. The man kept calling for help but no one wanted to take the risk of being killed or ending up caught there half alive. Unable to bear it any longer, my father dashed out, picked up the soldier and was nearing his own line when the explosion of a Russian grenade tore into his back. The trip to the hospital took him west towards the lines of the British and Americans. Ironically, his wounds undoubtedly saved his life.

My girlfriend had broken our engagement while I was imprisoned in France. In the meantime, she had met and married a local man who had sojourned in England as a German broadcaster of English propaganda. After the war he returned to Münster to work as a police detective.

After my visit with my mother I returned to the Hanau camp where I stayed on as a free worker. In June the barbed wire fence was taken down. With our greater freedom we soon learned that German money was worthless and that the gasoline in our trucks was priceless. We started selling five gallon containers of gasoline on the black market.

We had two 55-gallon fuel tanks on our trucks. When we filled up we didn't have to report how much we were taking, or how many miles we were driving. Sometimes I was driving 10 miles a day and I filled up my tanks twice. With gas you could buy anything. I purchased a new pair of shoes, and cloth, and even used gasoline to pay the tailor who made me a double-breasted suit. This was a risky enterprise because the Americans had tinted their gasoline with a red dye. A random stop by police that revealed red colored gas resulted in the automatic confiscation of a civilian vehicle.

One day the Military Police (MPs) came to our camp on the spur of the moment and made what we referred to as a *razzia*, a raid. We had established an early warning system and were aware of the oncoming jeeps. We grabbed the gas cans from under our floors, attached lines, the ends of which were secreted in the bushes bordering the river, and sunk them. The MPs searched everywhere, but they were unable to find any gasoline and left. As soon as they departed we recovered our cans and replaced them under the barracks.

In September I was nearly caught selling gasoline. They couldn't blame it on me because at the last moment I knew the area better than the American police and I was able to escape with my truck. Upon my return to camp I was called into the office. The interpreter said that they knew I was selling gasoline, but had been unable to catch me red-handed. His last words were, "You are dismissed."

I was presented with a voucher for 220 dollars. This was the money I had earned while working as a prisoner. I redeemed the voucher at a bank and was given 660 Reichmarks, the equivalent value of one pound of black market bacon.

Germany was in ruins. I married and began raising a family, all the while trying to discover the whereabouts of other 195th veterans. My photos were kept hidden from view, taped under the kitchen table. In 1955 Russia relented and allowed several thousand prisoners of war, a fraction of the hundreds of thousands captured, to return to West and East Germany. The others were never heard from again.

Eventually I lived in Quebec, Illinois, Hawaii, Washington state, and Florida. I had sought out, tested, and tasted adventure and now I find that even half a century later, everyday life is inseparable from the experiences that were so firmly imprinted on an impressionistic and youthful memory.